GOING ALONE

WOMEN'S ADVENTURES IN THE WILD

GOING ALONE

WOMEN'S ADVENTURES IN THE WILD

Edited by Susan Fox Rogers

SEAL PRESS

Going Alone: Women's Adventures in the Wild

Copyright ©2004 by Susan Fox Rogers

Parts of *Tough Girl* appeared in *Bitch* magazine, Issue 18.

Published by
Seal Press
An Imprint of Avalon Publishing Group Incorporated
1400 65th Street, Suite 250
Emeryville, CA 94608

Cataloguing-in-Publication data has been applied for.

ISBN 1-58005-106-5

9 8 7 6 5 4 3 2 1

Interior designed by Stewart A. Williams
Cover design by PDBD
Printed in the United States of America by Malloy Inc.
Distributed by Publishers Group West

Contents

To Alice

Introduction

GOING

1. a. The action of the verb Go, in various senses.
    1605 Shakespeare *Macbeth* III. iv. 119, Stand not upon the order of your going, But go at once. 1611 Beaumont & Fletcher *King & No King*, V. iv., Prayers were made For her safe going, and deliverie. 1868 G. MacDonald *Poems* 120, That moment through the branches overhead, Sounds of a going went. 1889 *Spectator* 16 Nov., Made happy by six thousand miles of continuous going.

    b. *esp.* Departure. Long going: departure on a long journey, i.e. death.
    1667 Milton *Paradise Lost* XI. 290, Thy going is not lonely; with thee goes Thy husband. 1792 Cowper *Letters* 30 July, Pray for us, my friend, that we may have a safe going and return.

    c. The faculty of walking.
    c1430 *Life of Saint Katherine* (1884) 37, By whos mighty vertu goynge is restored to the lame. 1635 E. Pagitt, *Christianography* III. (1636) 54, Life was given to the dead . . . going to the lame.

2. Manner or style of going; gait. In *pl.* of a horse: Paces.
    1674 Clarendon *History of the Rebellion* XI. 223, And the king all the morning found fault with the going of his horse. 1701 *London Gazette* No. 3703/4, A cropt Gelding . . . full aged . . . and all his Goings. 1805 Wordsworth *Waggoner* IV. 148, Erect his port, and firm his going.

3.   Means of access; a path, road; a passage, gangway (in a church).
     1715 Leoni *Palladios Architecture* (1742) I. 94, The going to the gal-
     leries . . . should have been by some few steps.

4.   a. Condition of the ground for walking, driving, hunting, or racing.
     Also, a line or route, considered as difficult or easy to follow;
     advance or progress as helped or hindered by the nature of the
     ground; *heavy going:* something difficult to negotiate; slow or diffi-
     cult progress.
     1848 Bartlett *Dictionary of Americanisms* 159, The going is good
     since the road was repaired. 1859 *Ibid* (ed. 2), Going, travelling; as
     "The going is bad, owing to the deep snow in the roads." 1884
     Baddeley & Ward *North Wales* 191, The going consists of stones
     and ruts concealed by heather to such an extent that almost every
     step is a matter of careful consideration. 1887 Sir R. H. Roberts *In
     the Shires* ii. 27, The fences are fair and the going pretty good,
     although the late rains have made it somewhat heavy. 1901
     Linesman *Words by Eyewitness* v. 101, A narrow path just above the
     waterline, overhung with bushes in parts, formed the "going." 1925
     E. F. Norton *Fight for Everest* 1924 114, we made very poor going,
     descending at a very much slower pace than we had made two years
     before. 1936 *Discovery* May 142/1, The next stage, up the North
     Ridge, is not very difficult technically but is, nevertheless, heavy
     going.

     b. *Colloq. Phrase* While the going is good: while the conditions are
     favorable; *freq.* To go while the going is good.
     1927 H. Waddell *Wandering Scholars* ii. 48, Warned in time, the two
     . . . had gone while the going was good.

ALONE

I. As an objective fact.

1. *lit.* Quite by oneself, unaccompanied, solitary.

   a. as extension of predicate.

   1601 Shakespeare *Julius Caesar* III. ii. 60, Good Countrymen, let me depart alone. 1611 Bible *Leviticus* xiii. 46, He shall dwell alone. 1807 Crabbe *The Parish Register* II. 409, Apart she lived, and still she lives alone. 1845 Ford *Handbook for Travelers in Spain* i. 43, It is almost impossible to travel alone.

   b. as complement to verb be.

   1382 Wyclif *Genesis* ii. 18, It is not good that a man be aloone or a woman. 1646 Howell *Letters* (1650) II. 121, I am never less alone, than when I am alone. 1798 Coleridge *Ancient Mariner* IV. iii., Alone, alone, all, all alone, Alone on a wide wide sea! 1851 Ruskin *Modern Painting* II. III. II. iii. 28, No man's soul is alone: Laocoon or Tobit, the serpent has it by the heart or the angel by the hand.

2. *fig.* a. Alone of its kind; having no equal, or fellow; being the sole example; unique; sui generis.

   1591 Shakespeare *Two Gentlemen of Verona* II. iv. 167, All I can, is nothing, To her, whos worth, make other worthies nothing; Shee is alone.

   b. Alone in action or feeling, having no sharer in one's action, or position.

   1752 J. Gill *Trinity* v. 97, Nor am I alone in the sense of this text. 1853 Thackeray *English Humorists of the 18th Century* i. 32, Through life he always seems alone, somehow.

3. To let or leave alone: literally to leave to herself; to leave persons or things as they are, to their own efforts; to abstain from interfering or having to do with.
    1850 Mrs. Stowe *Uncle Tom's Cabin* C. xx. 211, Topsy soon made the household understand the propriety of letting her alone; and she was let alone accordingly.

4. *attributive.* Said of that of which there exists no other example, or whose action is unshared in: Sole, only, unique exclusive. Now rare.

5. Take or acting by itself; of itself, without anything more.
    a. preceding the noun.
    Solitary, isolated, unattended.

    b. following the noun.
    1857 Buckle *Civilization* I. ii. 118, This fact alone must have produced a considerable effect.

    c. qualifying a possessive.
    1611 Bible *Romans* iv. 23, It was not written for his sake alone.

    d. separated from noun and tending to become adverb.
    1863 Kemble *Journal of a Residence on a Georgian Plantation* 19, Whose . . . perfect foliage would alone render it an object of admiration.

6. In all the preceding senses used also of a group or number: By themselves, without other companions.
    1824 Byron *Don Juan* II. clxxxviii., They were alone, but not alone as they Who shut in chambers think it loneliness.

II. As a subjective limitation.

7. With no one else in the same predicament; as distinct from any one else; only, exclusively. She alone came = she came, and no one else did.

a. immediately following the noun.
1854 Thackeray *Newcomes* I. xxi. 197, It is not youth alone that has need to learn humility.

b. Preceding or separated from the noun (hence tending to adverb).
1817 Coleridge *Sibylline Leaves* (1862) 125, That malignity of heart, which could alone have prompted sentiments so atrocious.

8. *adv.* Referring to verb, adjective, phrase, or clause: Only, solely, merely, simply, exclusively.
1850 Tennyson *In Memorium* cxiii., Wisdom . . . Which not alone had guided me, But served the seasons that may rise.

—*Excerpted and adapted from the* Oxford English Dictionary Online

White Rabbit

HOLLY KEITH

THIS BUNNY IS NOT GOING where I'm going.
I am in the White Mountains in winter, following bunny tracks in snow. The blazes that mark the trail below tree line are mostly masked by snow, and I am intuiting the way. The slope of the land, the space between trees, the quality of the snow, animal tracks. Bunnies often use the trails instead of hopping through snow-laden underbrush, but it is disconcerting how long I can follow the seemingly innocent prints before remembering that the bunny is not going where I'm going. As a general rule, bunnies do not like to summit. This one eventually veers left.

In a decade of hiking in the White Mountains, I have followed the tracks of rabbits and birds, foxes and deer, moose, and humans. I have followed my own tracks. I have purposefully not followed the tracks of a bear. This is the company in the Whites on a solo hike, the signs of others.

It is inadvisable to hike solo in the White Mountains in winter. A group of three or more is recommended.

This morning, unusual for winter, there was another car at the trailhead when I arrived. Three people, two men apparently preparing an adolescent boy for his first winter hike. As I stand up and pull my pack on, one man asks, "Are you with a group?"

I am standing alone next to my car, partially parked in a snowbank. There is my car; there is his car; there are just the four of us between this point and the horizon.

"I am not with a group."

I understand his desire to believe I'm not alone. He doesn't want to be responsible for me on the trail, and as a woman about to tag the summit alone I am probably taking the edge off whatever rite of passage he has planned for the boy.

He is taking the edge off my solo hike. In order to begin first, I fasten my pack and head off without checking snow conditions. The trail is unbroken, which will make the day more difficult both in finding the route and in kicking the steps for myself and for the men behind me. It will also make the day more beautiful, allowing me to see the landscape untrodden. Except by bunnies.

I hike only two hundred yards from the car before the depth of the snow necessitates snowshoes. They can be hard to walk in; they can be impossible to walk without. Even with snowshoes, I have sunk in the snow to my knees, to my thighs, and once, when the snow was deep enough to bury the trees, to my chin. I have learned to respect that which can swallow me whole. In the Whites, I carry snowshoes through the end of May, descending past women climbing in flip-flops on eighty-degree days who in under a mile from their air-conditioned cars will encounter five feet of snow. They look at me with cold curiosity. I look at them with warm feet.

I put my snowshoes on. It is 8:00 in the morning. I have been awake for four hours, driving for three. As mountains go, the Whites are short, with only one summit above 6,000 feet and tree line at roughly 4,000 feet. They are accessible. They are also deadly serious, and it is possible for most anyone to climb cavalierly into trouble. Hiking alone, I allow myself one mistake, other than the mistake of hiking alone. I can have trouble with one piece of gear, or the time, or the trail, or the weather, or myself. Combinations of two or more, even within a category, are cause for retreat. This is a good day. So far my level of error is having bought unfrosted Pop-Tarts. Doesn't count.

The recent snowfalls have loaded the trail and the trees. Everything is white, except the sky, which is an encouraging blue. Because of the snowpack, the trail is several feet higher than it is in summer, and branches intended to be above one's head are instead at face level. I empty the branches of snow with my ice axe before pushing through them. The temperature is relatively mild, below freezing but still double-digits, and the wind, at least below tree line, is light. For an hour or more the trail is a slow uphill climb. Occasionally I plunge the shaft of my axe into the snow for leverage. The way is not clearly marked but it is find-able, and I only have to check the compass once for a decision between two possible routes through the trees. I've set a general compass bearing ahead of time during the mapping of the trail, for rapid checks against total disorientation. Here in the calm of a clear ascent, I make a 180-degree adjustment on the reading, owing to the habit I have of making sure the compass always points to the car. It's okay to lose the way for-ward. It's not okay to lose the way back.

The bunny's and my paths diverge.

In the second hour, I arrive at one of those places of pure silence. I stop and listen to nothing for as long as nothing lasts. Sometimes it's interrupted by a bird, or by my heartbeat. Today it's interrupted by the wind, intermittent but howling, overhead.

I check the time. 8:25. Not right. This is my gear mistake, a new, untested watch, now frozen. I only wear a watch in the woods, where it offers one critical piece of information: when to turn back in the day even if the summit is still ahead. Alone in winter, I want to be done before dark, and the day is short. I feel as though I'm climbing well, but now that I can't tell if I'm late, I'll climb faster. After snacking. I pull on another layer just to grab half a Pop-Tart and some gorp from my pack.

Forward motion alone keeps the temperature bearable and rest stops have to be brief, and prioritized. One task per stop, a choice among eating, peeing, changing gear. I take my jacket off again to start climbing and put the pack back on.

What you carry matters as much as your ability to carry it. Gear matters. Weigh the gear against the risk. If your pack is too light you risk not having what you need; if it's too heavy you're more likely to need something. I am wearing boots and snowshoes. Wicking socks, vapor socks, hiking socks. Gaiters. Fleece pants with women's fly. Snow pants with women's fly. Two top layers plus a fleece jacket. Hat. Wicking gloves. Midweight gloves. A broken watch. I am carrying a pack with an energy gel bottle on my right strap and a water bottle on my left strap, with a compass and a whistle, just in case. I am carrying a rain jacket, balaclava, goggles, overmitts, an ice axe. A headlamp, and a spare microlight, just in case. Two quarts of water. Two insulated water bottle holders. Handwarmers. Gorp. Pop-Tarts, without frosting. Fig Newtons. A down jacket, a sleeping pad, and an emergency blanket, just in case. An extra vest, just in case. A fire-starting kit, a mug, and a knife, just in case. The map. Crampons. A screwdriver for the crampons, just in case. Toilet paper. Moleskin and one stretchy bandage, just in case. I am carrying the gene for Just in Case.

I have no stove, no sleeping bag. Every item brought and not brought is a decision. Each item brought is a string of decisions, and trials. One untested piece of gear per hike. What else one needs: luck, a turnaround time, the willingness to turn around at any time, and a trailhead holder, someone in the world who knows where you are and when you are supposed to be back. And, ideally in winter, more people. But it is not always easy to find people with gear and the desire to use it, and the decision becomes either to not climb or to climb alone. It's been suggested I assemble a group and lead a hike, but I won't bring anyone to a place I have not yet safely brought myself. And groups are not always safer. I have been in a group of eight at zero degrees with 90 m.p.h. wind gusts and in visibility so low that all I could see was the rear boot of the person before me, and that only sometimes. We were a blind parade, off the trail, with wind that could lift us and dash us against rocks in less time than it takes to say we're nothing but a pack of cards. Alone, I would have been somewhere else.

As I climb, the trees grow shorter. Before the trees stop I stop again and put on the wind jacket, the balaclava, the goggles, the overmitts. All day I've been expecting to share the summit cone with climbers who have ascended other trails. As I step above tree line and into the wind, I laugh. It's the laughter of having the world to myself.

I ascend snow and rock. There is still enough snow to be able to use snowshoes and not crampons, but its texture has changed, and I am no longer leaving a trail behind me. The snow looks petrified, frozen into waves and ripples. The trail here is marked by cairns, which are good for knowing that you are on the trail, but not always good for knowing which way you should walk to find the next one. I turn and study the way back. It snows a little from somewhere, literally out of the blue, but visibility is still good. The clouds are above. On some climbs, they're below. Sometimes they are right where you are. The wind is racing overhead, taking intermittent detours at my altitude. I think of the Whites above tree line as another planet. Or I think of it as back in time. It's old up here. I get so busy comparing the land above tree line to another place and another time, I sometimes forget that mostly it's like Earth, now.

The summit is a scramble. I climb to a view that it seems like only gods should get. I am surrounded by White Mountains earning their name.

This is the place where most climbing stories end. On the summit, wave the banner. But this is the halfway point, and the summit, the point you most want to get to, is the farthest you can be from safety. I start down.

Down is harder than up. On the ascent, choices narrow; uphill leads to the summit. Downhill leads everywhere. Plus I am not built for down.

I am resistant to the force of gravity, would rather push against than be pushed. The consequences of a mistake above tree line can be serious, have been, for some, fatal. I am close to the possibilities of danger here, but I am in no danger. I know where I am and where I'm going and I have what I need to get there. The potential danger is immense; the actual danger is low. I find the line between the two and follow it down.

On the way back I tag a lesser summit knob, a peak that doesn't officially count as one of the high peaks in the Whites, as there is not a 200-foot vertical drop between it and its neighbor. I always try for the lower summits, partly as a hedge against the day a new measurement comes out saying the lower knob is actually higher, partly because sometimes the lowly mountain neighbors are sweeter in either climb or view. This one offers me a view of where I've just been, which already seems distant.

I have not always loved mountains. Or winter. I had hiked in summer, with the sweat and the bugs and the tourists. A summit photograph from my first climb shows more than a dozen hikers seated, having lunch. I am standing in the middle, looking uninvolved, as though I'm waiting for the library to open. That winter I hiked with another group. We stayed out until the blue light of evening, the snow conditions perfect for glissading down the mountain, ice axe as rudder, the ice crystals on the trees sparkling by headlamp. I who loved neither mountains nor winter loved mountains in winter. I kept returning until late spring, when coming down from one climb I passed thirty-nine people assaulting the lower mountain without maps or jackets, emergency supplies, headlamps or compasses, or any clue as to the exalted season they had hibernated through. I stayed away until the snow fell again.

Below tree line, I meet the three hikers from the parking lot. They are resting on rocks, and pulling on clothes. The man who spoke to me earlier points to my snowshoes. "You sure can move in those things."

I nod. "They're good gear."

It's the gear. The magic snowshoes. Or maybe it's the time put in, the training, the gear and route research, the preparation. Regardless, he no longer seems concerned about my safety. I give him a weather report from the top and check my watch, which shows no time at all.

Some indeterminate number of hours before, while leaving the house, before dawn, in another state, with breakfast packed and trail food packed, and water, and snowshoes and axe, and sock systems and head-lamp, and maps to the trailhead and maps up the trail, there was a moment on the stairs when I thought, isn't this enough, haven't I earned the mountain just by knowing how?

The hiking is the easy part.

And the climb is a reward, which varies. The reward can be the silence. It can be a moose or a Canada jay. Sometimes on a many-mile hike it can be one step, one perfect step on a perfect day, placing a crampon into the perfect incline at the moment of a perfect view. Today the reward was the laughter, the sound of myself finding myself alone. And to have been, for a little while, alone. Self-contained. Self-sufficient.

"You sure can move in those things."

Yes. But of course it isn't the snowshoes at all. And he couldn't have pointed to what it really is that gets a person up a mountain, and down. Certainly your gear and your body, if you're lucky and you work at it, can take your mind places it couldn't otherwise go. But it doesn't happen unless your mind takes your body there first. What you need most is imagination, a willingness to step beyond the frame of the everyday, to follow the rabbit.

To climb a mountain is to commit an imaginative act.

I never learned this in summer, hiking in crowds. I suspected it in winter, watching others who knew. But I didn't learn it myself until all the tracks were gone, and I could enter wonderland alone.

Sharks

JODY MELANDER

M Y FRIEND LORI TELLS A STORY of growing up on Long Island, somewhere near Amityville where the *Jaws* movies took place. Her family owned a Sunfish sailboat, but never became proficient sailors. They'd set out in the morning, no particular destination in mind, drifting along the shore with the breeze behind them. It was not until the return trip that they'd realize they were in trouble. They'd try to tack, zigzagging upwind. After struggling all afternoon, making no headway and soaked by the waves, they'd usually abandon ship. Lori and her little sister would wait at the boat. Their father would head for the nearest house and ask to use the phone. He'd call Lori's mom, and she would sigh heavily and drive over in the family station wagon, rescuing them all yet again. An unusual twist to the tale: Lori's dad had only one leg. Since his prosthesis wasn't maneuverable in the small boat, nor were his crutches, he always left them behind.

Years later, Lori met a friend of a friend at a party. It turned out that he had grown up in the town next to hers. As they compared notes about their childhoods, she was astonished that the man had never learned to swim. "Why not? You lived right next to the ocean!" He told her it was because he was afraid of sharks. When he was a small boy, he said, just after the first *Jaws* movie was released, a stranger had shown up at his family's door, dripping wet and with only one leg. He'd never dared to go into the water again.

9

Unlike Lori, I grew up far from the ocean, in landlocked Central Pennsylvania, but like her, I grew up in a family that owned a boat. Tucked in a drawer somewhere in my parents' house is a photo that shows me as a budding sailor. It's taken in the early seventies, when I'm eleven or twelve, and in it I'm intently studying the rigging of the Mac Dinghy sailboat my family has just acquired. My father stands next to me, looking frustrated. Although we've spent the better part of the afternoon in the effort, we've finally eliminated all the spare parts—sorting through stays and halyards and sheets, and figuring out head and tack and clew. At last we know our daggerboard from our rudder. We've raised the mains'l and the jib, and the sails are filling with a light breeze. Despite our labors, though, we won't be going anywhere soon. In the picture, the boat sits on our front lawn, between the pachysandra beds and the dogwood tree. My youngest sister plays next to us in the freshly mown grass.

On summer Saturdays we'd hoist the Mac Dinghy onto the roof of our Buick, tie her down with a lumpy macramé of half hitches, and drive to one of the small man-made lakes near my hometown. She was a bathtub boat for a bathtub lake. Someone had warned us about the near impossibility of righting her if she ever "turned turtle" in a sudden gust. I worried, imagining my family clinging to the boat's round bottom and disappearing, one by one, mom, dad, two sisters, me last, as our fingers lost their grip in violent waves. Since we sailed only on hot and windless days, my fretting was unnecessary. The sun glared off the water. The air was filled with the buzz of cicadas in the trees on shore a few feet away from us. We'd sit in the bottom of the boat for an hour or two, swatting mosquitoes and making jokes about blowing into the limp sails. Then we'd give up. My parents would settle at a picnic table with wine and cheese, and my sisters and I would unstep the mast and pull out the oars to practice rowing and geometry. A straight line may be the shortest distance between two points, but we were much more proficient tracing the circumferences of circles.

With such an illustrious nautical background, it was probably inevitable that I'd make my home near the ocean. Twenty years ago, on my own for the first time, I traded the woods and mountains of Pennsylvania for Provincetown, Massachusetts, a strip of dune surrounded by sky and water at the farthest tip of Cape Cod. I was twenty-three, newly out, and I figured that this outermost and most outrageous place would be the best place to discover what that meant. That first terrified summer of my adulthood, I bought a plastic one-person inflatable rowboat, bright yellow to match my mood. I spent as much time as possible adrift in the harbor, trailing fingers and toes in the water, comfortable at sea and totally out of my depth on shore. Eventually I gained confidence and a local girlfriend. With permanent residence came a desire for less ephemeral craft, and I bought a kayak to paddle out into the harbor. Someone gave me a second kayak. Then, missing my early sailing years, I bought a used Sunfish with tattered rainbow-colored sails and patched orange and white hull. I cruised the bay for the next ten summers, practicing crisp racing turns, learning to sail backward as well as forward, hiking out over the water, thigh and stomach muscles taut, tanned bare feet hooked under the cockpit edge, losing swimsuit tops and sunglasses in unexpected capsizes.

Five years ago, my friend Jim called to offer me his boat, a Catalina 22 named *Beverly G* after his wife. "I'm not sure it's all that great a gift," Jim said. "It needs a lot of work," my friend the real Beverly added. They'd moved inland a few years before, leaving *Beverly* the Boat on the Cape, unable to take her with them, too nostalgic to sell her. I tried to sound thoughtful and mature. I said that I needed to think about it, but from the outset I knew there was no way I was going to turn down the offer. This, after all, was a real boat. I cast aside my old familiar Sunfish and fell for this new vessel as you might discard a faithful but all too familiar spouse for a fresh come-hither floozy in heavy eye makeup and a leopard-print teddy. I knew that she would require an exhausting amount of attention. I knew she was likely to prove difficult and fickle, a prima donna, probably heartbreaking, but I was so overwhelmed that something so lovely, so worldly, so out of my element could belong to me, that I didn't listen to my better judgment.

It was February when I got my first look at her, parked on her trailer at the ragged edge of an organic garden. From a distance she was very beautiful: tan hull, black boot stripe, red bottom paint. And very big: twenty-two feet, two thousand pounds. This was a far cry from my Sunfish. With *Beverly* I could take off and go places—leave the bay, sail across Nantucket Sound, visit Martha's Vineyard. I anticipated nights aboard, rocking in light swells, a lantern swinging gently on its gimbals. I could cook in her little galley. I could entertain friends—the boat slept four, according to the manufacturer (although boat manufacturers, like real estate agents, are inclined toward optimism). On closer inspection, she looked a little rough. She had no motor. Her trailer was rusty, the wheels frozen in place. Her keel winch was broken. Her scuppers had to be replumbed. There were two holes punched through her deck where someone had backed her safety rail into a tree. Her hatches were open and there was a foot and a half of icy water inside her. No matter, I was already smitten. So what if *Beverly* was a girl with lots of baggage? I told Jim I'd take her.

As in the case with all such relationships, the angst and weeping began almost immediately. First, whatever Beverly was, she wasn't cheap. My boat had many expensive needs. A motor, for instance. Long shaft or short shaft? Two-stroke or four? How many horsepower? I had no idea—I knew only that if I got into trouble in a vessel that weighed a ton, I wasn't going to be able to jump out and push as I had done with my Sunfish. I found an ad for a used Yamaha. Supposedly the previous, previous owner had been a boat mechanic. I should have heeded the inauspicious way that the electric start button came off in the seller's hand. Instead, I handed him $700 in cash and wrestled the motor into the bed of my truck. It weighed as much as I did. My new investment nearly always started, but was subject to dying unexpectedly. And not restarting. And always at a critical moment, as when the boat was going to go aground or run into a dock. Two years ago I finally broke down and bought a new, reliable motor. Another $1,500 on my credit card. Truth: A boat is a hole in the water into which you pour money. Variation: B.O.A.T. = Break Out Another Thousand.

With *Beverly*, I realized almost immediately that I was in over my head. That first year, for six months, through spring, early summer, mid-summer, late summer, I worked to get her ready for the water. I finally put her in, on the third try, the week before Labor Day, and pulled her out in a panic two weeks later just before a hurricane hit. Since I couldn't afford to hire anyone to help me, I had to learn to fix everything myself, but I was frequently so immobilized by anxiety and ignorance that I couldn't even look at the boat for weeks at a time. "What type of fiberglass should I use?" "What's a good bottom paint?" I interrogated yardmen at the marina, employees at boat-supply shops, the local harbormaster, hardware store clerks, colleagues at work, my car mechanic, strangers on the street, and anyone who looked as if he or she might know more than I did, which was pretty much everyone. And everyone had an opinion—often unfounded, always conflicting. As I stood in the aisle at the hardware store comparing product labels for hours at a time, the wrong choice seemed inevitable. And the wrong choice was sure to result in disaster.

Eventually I closed the holes in the deck—unaesthetically, but effectively, with fiberglass and gobs of marine sealant. I became a painter, squatting under the boat in the tall tick-filled grass, slopping on toxic bottom paint with a brush as baby mice fell on my head, disturbed in their nest above the swing keel. I became a mechanic of sorts, taking off the trailer's wheels, bashing out the old rusted brakes and repacking the bearings with thick yellow grease. Although the frozen wheels finally turned, the trailer's condition still worried me. I found that if I banged on the frame with a hammer, something I did fairly frequently in a sort of attraction-repulsion compulsion, big scabs of rusty metal fell onto the ground. I prayed everything would hold together on the ride to the launch ramp. The first year it all did. The second year, falsely secure, I pushed my luck too far. On launch day one wheel broke off, snapping from the axle as I drove. I had just time to pull to the side of the road before the trailer collapsed. Big boat, one-wheeled trailer. What could I do? I spent a frenzied day searching for a solution, which ultimately involved a second trailer, a forklift, three marina employees, two cops to direct traffic, and me. I paced next to the boat. Sometimes I clasped my hands in despair, and sometimes I remembered to look disconnected from the whole mess, a bystander disdainful of the incompetent jackass, who-ever he or she might be, who obviously had no business owning this boat.

In all the confusion, my friend Paul bailed me out repeatedly. He's a local boy—a fisherman, artist, jack-of-all-trades, and supremely self-sufficient. That first year, since I needed a dinghy, he showed me how he'd built his from two sheets of plywood and a few two-by-fours ripped lengthwise. I bought lumber and started sawing and hammering. The result was *Marge the Barge*. She's not a thing of beauty, flat-bottomed, boxlike, and a bitch to row in any sort of seas, but she's utterly functional, utterly dependable, and utterly stable. One fine day a few summers ago, Paul and I rowed *Marge* out into the harbor, Paul dressed in his usual ripped shorts, faded T-shirt, and Converse sneakers, me attired in bathing suit and ill-fitting wetsuit top. *Beverly's* keel cable was broken. With it bro-ken I couldn't winch up her keel, and with her keel dangling I wouldn't be able to get her onto a trailer at the end of the season. I had appealed to Paul. He dives for lobsters in the summer—could he dive under my boat and attach a new cable for me? He said he had a better plan.

When we reached *Beverly*, bobbing at her mooring behind the break-water, Paul helped me on with the rest of the scuba gear, sliding the backpack over my shoulders, strapping the tank in place. I felt clumsy and ungainly, off balance. Paul showed me how the regulator worked. I put it in my mouth and he turned the air on for me. "Breathe," he said. I breathed through the mouthpiece; everything seemed to be working. I spit into my goggles and swirled the saliva around to keep them from fogging, then put them over my face. I pulled on my borrowed flippers. "Okay," Paul said, "sit on the side of the dinghy—I'll balance us out on this side—then just fall backwards into the water." Uh-oh. I had taken the usual childhood swimming classes, but I had hardly been a star pupil. The teacher would throw her keys into the pool. Afraid to open my eyes under water, I would dive blindly, over and over, hands scraping the rough surface of the pool bottom, hoping to feel the irregular metal under my fingers. Eventually the teacher would get impatient and send some other more otter-like child in after me. Now weighed down with scuba tank and immobilized by neoprene, I was going to attempt another, more difficult, trick. I wasn't feeling very optimistic.

I like to tell Paul that I'm the son he never had. I say it because it amuses me and irritates him, but it does, in a way, characterize our relationship. Through the years I've known him, he's taught me to use a chain saw, mix concrete, jig for cod, shoot a .22. He shows me how to do boy things, and boy-like, I try not to whine or snivel or act frightened. So I sat on the dinghy's gunwale, as he'd instructed me to, held my breath, and splashed backward into the water. I didn't sink like a stone as I had feared, pulled under by the tank. The tight suit seemed to loosen slightly as it got wet. So far so good, I thought. As I held onto the dinghy's side, Paul reached over my head and turned my air on again and I put the regulator back into my mouth. We'd done this before. No sweat. But this time I had my mask on. This time I couldn't cheat and breathe through my nose. I was suffocating. Gasping, I spit the regulator out. "Try again," Paul said, and I finally began to get the hang of it. Inhale, exhale. Mouth, not nose. "Okay, now just swim under the boat and see how it feels."

I knew it was possible. I was, in fact, certain it was possible to immerse my head and body and breathe normally with the scuba tank. I ordered myself to move. Nothing happened. "Come on, you can do it." I was frozen, terrified, gripping the dinghy's side. "Come on." I dove suddenly, awkwardly downward, first holding my breath, then breathing quickly and shallowly. I tried to swim under the boat. Buoyed by the wetsuit, my arms and legs flailed ineffectively. As I passed into the dark water under *Beverly*'s hull, I felt myself being pushed upward toward the surface. But there was a boat in the way. My tank banged against the hull. What if I was trapped? I could feel my heart beating, pounding out of my chest. I was panting. My breath was impossibly loud. I turned and kicked frantically, bursting from the water, spitting out the regulator, tearing the mask from my face. Paul grabbed me by the handle of the backpack. "Okay?" He looked concerned, almost tender. I shook my head yes. "I think you'll be fine," he said, "but if you want me to do this for you, I will."

I might drown in the attempt, I thought, but I wasn't going to give up yet. This time I tried again with Paul's weight belt strapped around my waist. I held onto the dinghy until I'd regained my nerve. Then I dove. The panicky feeling returned immediately. But gradually I realized I didn't have to struggle, that with the weights I could stay under water easily. I could breathe with the tank and regulator. I calmed down, forcing myself to inhale and exhale steadily. I sounded like Darth Vader. This wasn't so bad. I reminded myself to open my eyes. My mask framed murky greenish water. As I turned toward the boat, I could see only *Beverly*'s red hull curving in front of me, but then I could make out her keel. A long looming wedge hanging under the boat, eight hundred pounds of cast iron, a fin. From its trailing edge dangled a frayed length of cable. I swam over to it, effortlessly hovered in the water. I removed the clevis and cotter pins that fastened the old cable to the keel. I fed a new length of cable up through the hull, through the reinforced rubber hose inside the boat, to the winch. I reattached the new cable to the keel with fresh pins. I had done it. I had only to wind the cable around the winch later, and the problem was fixed. In celebration, I swam away from the boat, kicking strongly with my flippered feet. I checked my mooring line, admired the creatures that had fastened themselves to it: mussels, sponges, knobby sea squirts. I breaststroked toward the bottom, looked at my mooring chain—no wear. My blocks sat solidly on the bottom. As I passed over them a startled tautog darted away. I resurfaced, and Paul said, "How'd it go?" "When can I come diving with you?" I asked.

On launch day this year, Tim, my "boat guy," drove up from Orleans with his big hydraulic trailer, smoothly maneuvered Beverly off her stands, and drove her to the ramp at the West End parking lot. I followed behind in my truck, watching her swaying and bouncing high above the road. For the first time I hadn't needed to do any major repairs, just a little touchup and painting. My friends Laine and Sally waited as we pulled into the lot, there to give moral support and to help step the mast, although neither had time for a sail. We climbed to Beverly's deck and unbungeed the mast from the rails. We lugged the butt end aft and placed it on the deck plate. Then, walking forward, hands on the thick aluminum shaft, leaning and leveraging like soldiers with the flag at Iwo Jima, we tipped the mast perpendicular. We reattached the forward shrouds and the forestay, tightened the turnbuckles, and rigged the boom. My crew clambered down. Tim slowly backed the trailer down the ramp, the water swirling first around the trailer's tires, then its thick metal frame, then finally around Beverly's freshly painted hull. With a slight swaying and a clanging of halyards against the mast, she settled into the familiar element, a duck ruffling her feathers, rearranging her wings, floating in the water. I started the motor, shifted into reverse, and Beverly slid smoothly into the bay. Sal and Laine waved from shore. Tim pulled away with dripping trailer. Another season begun.

From the launch ramp at the West End parking lot, Provincetown harbor curls farther west, then south, then east, ending in a spit of sand marked by a small white lighthouse. This is Long Point, the outermost tip of the Cape. I steered for the open waters beyond it. My boat was successfully launched. My motor hummed. It was a beautiful day and I had no place to be.

Late in the afternoon the winds sometimes die completely, and the sea becomes glassy, the water's surface silver and viscous like mercury. The bay stretches flat, horizontal—a vast lateral expanse. White clouds overhead, puffy cumulus, wispy cirrus, are reflected in this mirror, slightly distorted by the dimples and bulges of tiny swells. Along shore there are two rows of houses, two lines of dunes, two tall images of the Pilgrim Monument, the solid, familiar right-side-up versions, and their otherworldly, shimmering reverse. Everything is visible for miles: a gull sitting far off on the water's surface; a distant buoy; a fisherman long-lining for fluke, his orange dory a bright trapezoid, thin oars pointing skyward. A cormorant flies past, low to the water, wingtips wetted with every beat, feathers whistling. In one small area, the vast, still mirror is broken as tiny baitfish leap, raining down on the water, and bigger fish come from below in pursuit, roiling and flashing.

It was under these conditions that I saw the fin. It was a long way off, toward the Truro shore, but it was unmistakable. A solid black triangle jutting from the bay. It wasn't a dolphin or whale's fin, I decided. I've seen both from boats before and this was the wrong shape, and there was something about the way it moved steadily through the sea that seemed cold-blooded and fishlike rather than mammalian. I pointed the bow toward the mysterious creature, gave the motor some gas. Excited, I figured I was probably looking at a basking shark, which I'd heard about from Paul and others, but had never seen before. They're huge, and harmless, and often come into the bay in the summer, filtering plankton with their great gummy mouths. As the motor chugged along and the distance closed, I got a better view of the fin, moving slowly and rather aimlessly along the water's surface. It had to be at least four feet high. A monster fish. When I was perhaps thirty feet away, I put the motor into neutral and went forward. I stood on deck, holding onto the mast, looking at the beast in the water ahead. The boat's momentum carried me closer. Initially the shark swam in front of the boat, slowly, not changing course, but as I came up on it, it unhurriedly dove under my bow. I caught a glimpse of a huge gray body, as big around as a Volkswagen bus, a triangular dorsal fin, a lobed tail fin. Then it disappeared into the dark water.

Drifting, I waited for a few minutes, then five, then ten, hoping the shark would resurface. I knew it could not be far away. I marveled at the way that such a huge creature could vanish so completely. In the shadow of my boat, I saw a few blades of eelgrass floating near the surface, and a couple of nearly invisible, gelatinous comb jellies. Only the top few feet of water were transparent. Below was green-black and opaque. How many hundreds of feet of this black water lay between me and the bottom? What else besides the basking shark swam beneath me? As I looked around, I realized that in this area of the bay, a mile at least from any land, on a calm, hot July day the previous summer, I had gone swimming with a couple of friends. We'd sat becalmed in my boat for several hours, chatting, sipping beers, baking in the sun, perfecting torsos without tan lines. Then one by one we'd jumped over the side into the cold sea, treading water as the empty boat rocked beside us. None of us had given any thought to creatures that might be lurking below. I didn't think I'd ever be quite so unconcerned again.

At last, I put the outboard into gear and turned back toward town. The shark was gone, but I could at least say I'd seen it for a moment. My motor vibrated steadily. I stood in the cockpit, looking forward. I steered with the end of the tiller pressed into the small of my back, shifting my weight from one foot to the other to make course adjustments. I held onto the sailboat's boom, both hands above my head, relaxed, stretching. *Beverly* cut smoothly through the water. I watched the bow wave vee out beside her. Idly I looked behind me to where the shark had been. Empty water. No, the fin was back.

Taking the tiller in my hand, I started to turn the boat toward the shark again, but then I hesitated. Something was different. This time the fin was coming toward me. It no longer seemed aimless, but was deliberately moving through the water, and moving fast. I started to wonder. Was this really a basking shark? I remembered Paul telling me how a friend of his had been fishing off the backside behind Wellfleet this spring. Sitting in his boat, line over the side, he'd heard the smack of something very large hitting the water's surface, and turning around, he'd seen rings of concentric circles expanding near him. He kept looking, wondering what it was. Then a seal came flying out of the waves, leaping, frantic. And behind it came an enormous shark, open jaws filled with sharp teeth.

The fin was getting closer. I didn't like how it looked. A black triangle gliding purposefully, a cartoon, a cliché of a shark. I remembered how big the beast had been below my boat. I had visions of being attacked, *Beverly* torn to pieces one splintery bite at a time, me scrambling across the deck, crying out, trying to stay ahead of the lunging creature. Finally having nowhere else to go. I could almost hear the "dun dun, dun dun, dun dun . . ." of the music from *Jaws*. I reached for the motor, turned the throttle as high as I could, and sped away as fast as my boat would take me, my heart racing almost as fast as the motor. The fin receded, eventually disappeared.

I motored toward Long Point. Just off the point is a green bell buoy, a floating drum topped by metal scaffolding, to which are fixed clappers and a bell. It clangs irregularly as it rocks in the waves. As I drew closer to it, I saw another fin, then another, and another. A total of seven. All huge. I felt a little wave of panic, but told myself to calm down. It was possible there was one Great White in the bay, I decided, but seven? Eight including the one I'd seen earlier? I couldn't imagine it. I steered closer. I couldn't tell what the sharks were doing. Feeding? Mating? Some cruised along by themselves. Three sharks swam together near the surface, their back and tail fins in line—big dorsal, smaller caudal, big dorsal, another caudal, third dorsal, final caudal—looking like the jagged back of some enormous serpentine sea monster. I shut the motor down, drifting, not wanting to disturb them.

One fin changed course and moved toward my boat. I reached for the starter cord on my motor. Oh lord, why had I shut it off? I stopped myself. Told myself to relax. As the shark came near I could see its huge leathery head, mottled gray, somewhat wrinkled-looking, its body, nearly as wide as my boat, its dorsal fin jutting from the water, its tail fin sweeping steadily back and forth. It surfaced just a few feet behind me, blunt nose first. It opened its gigantic mouth. I pulled back. But it was toothless, white-gummed. A basking shark. As I watched, it spread its gills, like an umbrella opening. They gaped wide, white inside, almost encircling its head. It was feeding.

For the next twenty minutes the beast floated behind and beside my boat, white maw yawning wide, head distended, inflated. Monstrous. At times I could have touched it. I wondered how the skin would feel, but I didn't dare to find out. I leaned on the rail, still, watching in amazement. Why had it come up to me? Was the water flowing along the hull of my boat concentrating the plankton on which it was feeding? Did it think Beverly was a beautiful lady shark? Sometimes it's tempting to interpret animal sightings metaphorically: the real animal carrying out its normal activities juxtaposed with a messenger spirit. The great horned owl, say, that appears day after day in the same patch of woods, drifting silently through the trees, alighting on a branch with out-stretched talons. Is this just coincidence? Or a reminder to be aware of hidden dangers? What was the message offered by the basking shark? I thought of all the effort that had gone into making *Beverly* seaworthy, all the fears I'd had, how they'd proved to be unfounded, and how I'd over-come each one. Now here I was, alone, competent, witness to a marvel. Maybe my basking shark was reminding me to celebrate.

I watched the feeding shark for a while longer, awed and joyous. At last I looked up, realizing the day was ending. The sky behind the mon-ument was turning orange. I was far offshore with no running lights. I needed to move, before it got too dark to find my mooring. Not want-ing to disturb or injure the shark as I started my motor again, I banged on the side of the boat. "Come on, beautiful, time to go." It seemed to understand, closed its mouth, pulled ahead. It swam forward, its tail even with my stern and its head at my bow, twenty-odd feet away. Then, like the first shark, it dove under the bow and vanished. I pulled the starter cord on my outboard once, then a second time. It caught and growled steadily. I turned toward town. Behind me Long Point glowed in soft yellow light, the bell buoy clanged, and the sharks swam.

Walking

GRETCHEN LEGLER

THE HELICOPTER HOVERED over the rugged, ice-carved mountaintop, whipping up gravel and sand. A hunched figure came running from a tent nearby, clutching a hat to its head. Out of the open helicopter door was handed a cookstove, which the figure grabbed under its arm, then there were waves of the hand and nearly inaudible shouts of thanks, and we lifted again, the tiny camp below us diminishing to no more than bright dots of color in the sweeping landscape of ice and stone.

I was in Antarctica, along for a morning helicopter ride with McMurdo Station technician Tracy Dahl. Dahl had flown to the Lake Hoare science camp in the Dry Valleys, where I was spending the week, and together we had choppered up the Taylor Valley. Dahl was to deliver the stove and other supplies to two graduate students who had pitched their peaked yellow canvas Scott tents on the top of a windy, gravelly, high plateau. The next stop was a pickup and delivery at Lake Bonney, farther up the valley, and then, finally, Dahl and I were to set down outside the three uninhabited canvas Jamesways that made up the Lake Fryxell Camp, which Dahl was to prepare for a soon-to-be-arriving field party.

Antarctica's Dry Valleys are the world's coldest desert—a landscape so alien that it had become a testing ground for equipment the United States hoped one day to send to Mars. That I was here was due to the generosity of the U.S. National Science Foundation's Artists and

Writers Program, a program that offers fellowships for musicians, poets, novelists, photographers, painters, and children's storytellers, who all want to travel to this faraway land and make what sense they can of it in their own evocative tongues.

I had come to Antarctica for many reasons, some more consciously realized than others. To travel to this terra incognita was a longtime personal dream and a momentous professional opportunity for me as a writer. But I had deeper reasons, too, one of which a friend pointed out to me before I left: "You're going to come face to face with yourself," she said. Perhaps I wanted to come face to face with myself and see what I saw; see what the landscape of ice and stone could reveal to me about who I was, what earth I stood upon, what made me, and what fixed me to the places, people, and ideas I held most dear. A more profound adventure I could never imagine.

After the chores were complete Dahl and I sat beside the fuel stove in one of the Jamesways and warmed our feet on its metal sides, tipped back in our chairs, drinking tea, passing the time until his helicopter arrived to take him back to McMurdo. Then I would be on my own. I was equipped for a small expedition: radio, backpack with tent, stove, sleeping bag, extra food, and clothes. I would make my way back on foot to Lake Hoare, the field camp where I had been staying for the week. Mine was an officially sanctioned several-hour walk. If I did not arrive at Lake Hoare by dinnertime, a helicopter would probably be sent from McMurdo to find me. Nevertheless, it felt like an adventure—a walk in Antarctica, a walk in the wildest place I had ever been, a walk in what might yet be the wildest place on Earth.

Every walk, said Henry David Thoreau, that nineteenth-century American saunterer of woods and mind, is a sort of crusade—a westward going, a wildward going—a journey toward self-awareness, transformation, and the future. We should be prepared, he said, on even the shortest walk to go "in the spirit of undying adventure, never to return—prepared to send back our embalmed hearts only as relics to our desolate kingdoms." The name itself, walker, saunterer, Thoreau wrote, may have derived from the expression used to describe a person in the Middle Ages who wandered about the land, à la Sainte Terre, a pilgrim, heading toward the Holy Land. Or it might be rooted in the words sans terre, without a home, but everywhere at home.

I felt both as I set off across Lake Fryxell, my ice axe swinging like a walking stick at my side, its metal point pinging against the hard turquoise surface beneath me. The teeth of my crampons bit in as I walked: metal against ice. The blue lake ice was cut by geometric patterns of crazy white lines and rising white orbs. I felt homeless and at home in the universe, and as if I too were a pilgrim, walking not toward, but in, a holy land.

The flatness of the valley I was in was broken on each side by distant hills swathed in shades of brown and white, the ones to my back more mountainous and sharp, and the ones facing me, softer. My way led across Lake Fryxell, so beautifully disturbed by the designs in its frozen surface, toward the edge of the Canada Glacier, which spilled out of the mountains between Fryxell and Lake Hoare and which I would have to go around. I paused frequently on the walk, gazing, enthralled with patterns in the snow made by wind, so delicately and improbably shaped— like letters, like words, like whole sentences written in dark brown dust on snow. Often I would stop to simply gaze about me, down the valley where it spread out wide and met the blue and white cloud-spattered sky, behind me to see the tiny Jamesways of the Fryxell camp receding, and the towering glacial wall, emanating coldness. Many times, when I paused, the glacier would crack and thunder and I would jump for fear that I would be smashed by a falling chunk of ice as big as a house, me like a fly beneath it.

Such congenial openness I had never walked in, never traveled by foot in such intimacy with. One step at a time would take me back to Lake Hoare by evening. Each step I savored, giddily feeling my strong legs hinge at the hips, feeling each stride, my lungs expanding fully, my arms swinging, my back bearing the weight of the pack. I felt as Thoreau did when he wrote, "In my walks I would fain return to my senses." The land here was bare bones, stripped down, elemental, and beautiful; beautiful in the way the bleak, landless, endless ocean is beautiful to fishermen; the way deserts are beautiful to Saharan nomads; beautiful in its smallness—the many-colored pebbles in my path, the ragged ice along the shore, the turquoise glass I walked upon; and beautiful in its largeness—the infinite reach of sky, the gigantic arc of the land. The land brought me back, as it did Thoreau, to my senses; back to my body, back to my self.

As I walked I pondered how the world was reached through the self, how the universal comes of the particular, the immense from the intimate. Thoreau called it "recreating self," and for it he went to the most dismal of places; he entered the darkest of woods, the swampiest of swamps; they were his sacred places, sanctum sanctorum—for they were the places that were truly wild. What would he have made, I wondered, of Antarctica?

The woods and meadows of nineteenth-century New England were Thoreau's wilderness. He called it a mythic land: "You may name it America, but it is not America; neither Americus Vespucius, nor Columbus, nor the rest were discoverers of it. There is a truer account of it in mythology than in any history of America." That he walked in a mythic landscape meant to him that his journey took him into all time. Thoreau walking in his woods, me walking alone from Lake Fryxell to Lake Hoare, around the booming edge of the towering Canada Glacier, was humankind, womankind, mankind walking, walking in an unknown land. You may name it Antarctica, but it is not Antarctica. All moments converge here in this place and time—all efforts at renewal, all quests for knowledge, all attempts at transformation and adventure collide here in this *solid* earth, in this *actual* world.

As I rounded the final protruding hunk of ice of the Canada Glacier and came within sight of the Lake Hoare camp, I could see the tiny purple, blue, and yellow dots of the domed tents, and the glint of the sun off the small metal buildings. I pulled my radio out of the bulging deep pocket of my bibbed wind pants and called in. "W-002 calling Lake Hoare," I said, giving my Antarctic code name, the W standing for Writer. The radio crackled and popped and then came the familiar voice of Bob Wharton, the principal investigator at the camp. "Roger, this is Lake Hoare Camp. How would you like your steak done?" It would be good to be back among them, but it had been better to be out alone, walking in Antarctica, feeling that magical, paradoxical diminishment of self and enlargement of spirit that such a landscape brings—that feeling that one is in the presence of something that has been in existence long before you and will continue long after you, into all time; some spirit that is larger and older than the human mind, and that, in its power, comforts rather than terrifies, soothes rather than agitates.

"I believe in the forest, and in the meadow, and in the night in which corn grows," wrote Thoreau. This is what he crusaded for, what he walked for—the *common sense*, the link between spirit and body, Earth and self. I believed in this too—that there was a sublime power in this land that could mysteriously help a person reconnect with that subtle magnetism in wildness that would show her the way. I believed in this vast glacier-scoured landscape, this thundering ice, and in the impossible simplicity of the thin line between the frozen earth and sky.

In the Tracks of Old Ones

GENEEN MARIE HAUGEN

It WAS EIGHTY-EIGHT DEGREES in the shade when I locked the car and staggered toward the trail with my dogs. They had big paws and cold noses, but it was all disguise. I knew their true identity: happiness in fur coats. In minutes, they were wet from chasing sticks in the snowmelt creek. They smelled like something returned from the dead. Emmy had already bucked wildly and thrown off her new pack. Now she twisted her golden head to eye the red saddlebags with suspicion, then sprinted ahead as if to outrun them. Flipper was an old backpacking dog and endured his modest load with patience. My knees buckled from the weight on my back although it was far less than I once could carry. I considered soaking my tie-dyed shirt in Darby Creek before we started climbing, but it was sweat-saturated in minutes. I couldn't imagine how I'd endure both the load and the heat. For a second I wondered why—if you didn't count the dogs—I'd chosen to go solo. There was no reasonable answer to this question.

It would not be the first time I'd wandered off without any explanation other than knowing it was time to go—which can be the most treacherous reason of all. Hearing the call to adventure, however small or grand, carries a twofold danger: successful resistance requires a psychic numbing, but succumbing to the call opens the awful door to the unknown, which is hardly (as most of our mothers would caution) a sensible choice.

Veering purposefully onto an uncertain path usually doesn't make any rational sense until later, and maybe not even then.

Deer flies and mosquitoes hovered around us, biting the dogs' noses and my bare legs and arms. All three of us were panting within minutes. Normally, Flipper and Emmy were enthusiastic about almost anything, but now they sat down on the trail and turned to look at me as if I were crazy.

Maybe I was.

But generally, I was not influenced by the disapproval of dogs.

A low approval rating from the culture, however, was another matter, and one I'd yet to completely accept—or ignore.

Less than a mile from the trailhead we crossed into the Jedediah Smith Wilderness, where the route switchbacked through the green shade of old Douglas fir and lodgepole. Emmy wanted to lead, and she rammed me in the back of the knees with her pack every few minutes as she passed, and then got distracted by some irresistible off-trail odor. The heart-piercing song of a hermit thrush drifted down from the canopy. The heat-blasted air was redolent with hot pitch. I sweated and climbed and sucked from the tube leading to the reservoir attached to my pack, not caring that the water was warm and tasted like plastic.

Two hikers approached from the opposite direction. "Hello," I said, stepping aside to let them pass. They walked by without a glance toward me, without a word, as if I were not standing inches away.

The trail left the shade and traversed west-facing, sun-baked slopes colored more outrageously than tie-dye by lupine, pink geranium, purple penstemon, yellow balsamroot, crimson paintbrush, creamy columbine. I have taught myself the names of wildflowers, though I can't always identify what's growing from newly emerging leaves. If a plant doesn't blossom conspicuously, I might not notice it at all. But if, over the years,

I see a flower that I've never found in a field guide, I feel at a loss, as if recognition is incomplete without a name.

Sometimes a name I've taken such care to learn disappears into a sinkhole of memory. It's almost worse than misplacing the name of a dear friend at a party, where it's possible to prevent public mortification and recover the lost name through elaborate social maneuvering. In the mountains, it's only the nameless flower and myself, waiting for the name to surface again. It had once taken days to resurrect "self-heal." I recognized the familiar damp-habitat blossoms, but—inarticulate—felt as if I'd lost something more than common language.

My once-chiseled memory was no longer neatly delineated; it was labyrinthian and winding, with drop-offs, dead ends, and sudden resurgences, and I could not navigate in my customary, straightforward, confident manner. I had to stalk missing pieces of memory in a newly subtle way, as if looking out the corner of an eye, or through a blurred window that only suggested the shape of what was beyond the pane.

The name "self-heal" had returned suddenly, in a daydream.

After a while, the dogs and I developed a routine. With puppy enthusiasm, Emmy charged ahead to the next spot of shade and sprawled out. Flipper waited for me to say it was okay to rest there. I turned to face whatever breeze cooled my sweat-soaked body. When we all stopped panting, we stepped back into the sun. We climbed a thousand feet. It must have been cooler, but I couldn't tell.

The trail was paved in places with limestone: wrinkled and porous as skin. A white plume of water fell between the splayed flanks of the pale canyon. Shadowed clefts in the farther wall marked other entrances to the stone mountains. It's tempting to think of dark damp caverns as feminine, but I usually resisted the impulse. For me, the Mother-Earth, Father-Sky metaphors were too simple, too polarized, too . . . *diminished* by gender division.

I was thinking about gender, though, and about age, and about how age seems to affect women and men differently, influenced by hormones and cultural roles, complicated further by the quirky genetic pool, complicated again by our own expectations and imaginations—the frame through which we perceive ourselves sprinting or limping toward the future.

Age was part of the hazy reason I'd chosen to slog uphill in an inferno with only dogs for companionship. Wild, silent, solo time was a good fantasy for someone who'd been long-partnered with an outdoor kind of guy: dreaming of wilderness trips I'd do alone was kind of like flirting outside the relationship but never consummating. I hiked and skied by myself, naturally, but overnight in the backcountry was the boundary I'd turned back at for more than a decade.

I had a little anxiety about this. Not about camping alone, but about a vague sense of loss: loss of strength, courage, youthful grace, some culturally sanctioned semblance of beauty. Who knew if the years ahead would be kind? Knees, hips, and fingers already swelled and stiffened without warning. The margin of time for everything I'd been postponing until later was shrinking with alarming rapidity. Later now loomed so close that there was a possibility of staggering blindly right past it, with no chance for return.

I was already witnessing how some women my age were extricating themselves, in increments, from the outdoor experience. First, no more swimming naked; then, no more submerging the face or hair. First, no more backpack trips without a man. Then, no more backpack trips at all. Then, no more sleeping on the ground. Then, no more sleeping outdoors. I was terrified that this would happen to me, this slow and seemingly inevitable closing down that apparently had less to do with physical ability than with preset cultural programming.

A woman who'd heard I was going backpacking asked, "Geneen, how *old* are you? Don't you remember how *hard* that is?" I couldn't bear to believe that a time would arrive when what I remembered about large or small adventures was that they had been difficult, uncomfortable, or frightening, when I forgot that joy had always balanced, if not outweighed, the pain.

Once, years ago, when my friend and river mentor Michael returned from guiding and sea kayaking in Papua New Guinea, he came to the Santa Cruz house I inhabited at the time and told me how he'd been ambushed by natives in tribal dress who resented outsiders on their rivers; how he'd been accosted at sea by law enforcement agents with dubious credentials. When Michael left, I considered my comfortable home and life and thought: I've got to do something; *I'm turning into a suburban housewife*. I ran to the beach and dove under the breaking waves. It was Spring Equinox, the ocean was frigid, but I made myself swim with the otters and seals until my body was numb. It wasn't Papua New Guinea, it wasn't even exotic. It must have been miserably cold, but my body carries a memory of shedding a too-tight skin, loosening the boundary of ordinary experience.

The body itself largely determines how fluidly one moves into age. Even the best-kept joints and muscles (which mine certainly were not) creak and tear. But more injurious is the atrophied imagination, when what we believe about ourselves becomes too small.

Tumbling off the limestone wall in the distance, the waterfall surprised me, made me think we were *almost there*. I lurched ahead in anticipation. Then I saw water falling from the dark cavern even higher and realized we still had a thousand feet in elevation and perhaps a couple of switchbacking, uphill miles to walk. It is not a far distance or hard ascent with a hip pack in cooler temperatures, but I was lugging a tent, sleeping bag, colder-weather clothes, food, stove, first aid, journal, and hardcover book. The dogs carried their own food, the fuel bottle, water purifier, and my sandals. I carried about one-third of my body weight on my back; the dogs, probably one-eighth. Even so, they eyed me sideways, accusingly.

I remembered how camping solo—once I'd gotten over the conditioned, initial terror—had made me feel I'd found home, both in the world and inside myself. Although some denizens of proper urban enclaves regarded me as a little deviant, the outdoor forays hadn't made me feel at all like an aberration, but like myself, more fully expressed. I felt some of that fullness eroding now, vanishing at the edges like wildflowers in a hard freeze.

I no longer went to the mountains in search of conquest, a common pursuit of youth. I traveled now welcoming the inevitable, temporary panic over leaving a comfortable home, the terror that home is as fragile as the belongings I carry—and as monumental as the world. I traveled anticipating the subtle downshifting of mind. I traveled welcoming silence and whatever fears might rise as night falls. There was also, as always, a longing for something else I couldn't name.

A family approached, walking down the trail. "Hello," I said. Two children stepped around me, heads down, without a sound. The parents kept their eyes on the children and were likewise silent.

I was beginning to wonder if I were becoming invisible.

Five hikers and three dogs emerged from the dark surging mouth of the Wind Cave. They didn't carry lights; they couldn't have gone far. One of the hikers slipped in the torrent of water. He recovered before falling off the canyon wall, but who needed to see more? I was no longer totally reckless. The opening was too flooded and fast to enter alone. The cavern was serious, a limestone honeycomb. A series of passages led to the Wind Cave from the Ice Cave farther up canyon, but to travel between the two required technical climbing skills, crampons, rappelling equipment, fail-proof lights and directions, winter clothes, and possibly a wetsuit for the icy floods—far more navigational hazards than in the labyrinth of my eroding memory.

It's said by some that the Teton Range, of which these caves were part, contain artifacts from the lost continent of Atlantis. The caves may hide flying saucers, for all I knew, never having been inside, but the surrounding rocks are studded with fossils that predate Atlantis. These mountains, rising some two and one-half miles above sea level, were once a primordial ocean floor, and lifted in inverse fortune to the fabled continent.

I stepped around chunks of limestone embedded with radiating, fossilized disks. Some boulders were encrusted with pale, striated tubes. Milky geode-like crystals. Rust-colored spirals. I couldn't pass by so casually. The dogs were relieved when I pulled their packs off and shrugged off my own for a rest beside the small stream.

I tried to hold this in mind: In the history of this land, an immense shudder shot the Tetons into the air, wore off the Paleozoic and Mesozoic coverings, exposed the Precambrian gneiss and schist, and uplifted the limestone where I now sat, once the bottom of a warm-water sea. Glaciers crept through, slow-motion rivers of ice. Streams flowed through the limestone, carving caves and passageways. Just to the north, a great volcano, the Yellowstone caldera, repeatedly, regularly erupted, burying successive forests, covering the plains of Kansas with ash.

I tried to hold this all in mind, but I had no reference for such unimaginable change. In fact, I was completely undone, dizzy, trying to imagine such upheavals and transfigurations of Earth, educated, as I am, in a culture with little regard for the nonhuman past and little vision for the future. Even while surrounded by evidence of endless (and often cataclysmic) metamorphosis, contemporary humans live as if entitled to the unlimited, perpetual bounty of a hospitable Earth.

And we have created a culture of perpetual adolescence—a culture that mistakes immaturity for youthfulness.

· · ·

Weary and wandering off-trail, I found a place to camp in the shade near a small, fast stream. When the tent was up, I investigated the stream and found it originated as a gushing spring, pouring out of a crack in a limestone basin. I considered my filter, and I decided that if this spring, filtered through stone, was not pristine, no water on Earth is. I filled my water bottle and drank half of it at once. Filled it again.

Maybe a certain disorientation brought on by heat and exertion gave the spring more metaphoric significance than it actually had, but the water pouring out of the rock made me unreasonably happy: Sometimes, the life that goes underground reappears again, perhaps clarified by the time of invisibility.

In the contemporary world, women of midyears are expected—encouraged—to disappear, to be, perhaps, subsumed by the generic role of mother, to cease being unique, interesting, or sexually appealing. With only a few recent exceptions, Hollywood (the principal reflector/creator of cultural norms) is notorious for the invisibility of independent, sensual, strong, intelligent women beyond, say, thirty-five. And in motion pictures and other media, one particular image of Western womanhood—the outdoor-oriented female—hardly exists at all, and certainly not at midlife.

At a mountaineering shop where I'd been a regular customer for twenty years, I'd noticed, lately, how the young saleswomen—athletic mountain beauties—had carried on conversations about climbing with each other whenever I'd come in. For some time now, not one had asked if I needed assistance, or even appeared to notice when I was in the shop. I suppose one adapts to being a cellophane-woman, but I wasn't there yet, and I was still surprised—no, shocked—to find that if I approached, the clerks would eye me skeptically, as if to ask: What could *you* possibly need in a mountaineering store? A woman might be accustomed to dismissal from a "go big or stay home" kind of man, but these youthful Amazons did not seem to realize the trail had been partially broken for them by older women adventurers—women who might, in fact, still occasionally need a topo map or a new pair of boots for a hobble into the wildish world.

But I had to admit I had been equally naive.

The female explorers ahead of me had been nearly invisible, barely represented in any media—recreational or otherwise—seldom celebrated, hardly known outside their own small fields. You had to work to discover them. Ask questions. Trace hints of stories. In such a way I found out about the bikini-clad crone-guide of the Colorado River, Georgie White; in such a way I found out about Alaskan bush pilot Celia Hunter; in such a way I found out about the first European woman in Lhasa, Alexandra David-Neel. All had wandered way off the culturally approved trail, and only by wandering off-trail myself could I find their tracks.

I expected to be a little afraid, or lonely.

The dogs and I walked up the ridge, bade farewell to the sun.

The stars accumulated.

Subalpine fir rocked in the night wind.

The stream rushed past with a loud gasp, like a diver coming up for air.

I woke often, cramped by the dogs' weight, Flipper stretched over my legs, Emmy's head on my chest. I was sleeping in the forest among animals. Two of them, it's true, were my familiars. But when their furred ears lifted in response to sounds I couldn't hear, I suspected they were just humoring me and could abandon domestic comforts and rejoin their wilder relations any time.

The night was gentle. Birds stirred with the first gray light.

There was no fear or loneliness.

I had not brought a hairbrush or comb on purpose. I'd not brought clean clothes on purpose. I had not brought coffee on purpose, which turned out to be an excellent decision since the stove I'd brought for tea malfunctioned. None of these things were much to let go of for twenty-four slightly less-civilized hours. Twenty-four hours was not much time, just what was "available" for this barest peeling away of culture.

The alarmed, chirping marmots didn't care that my hair was not groomed. No one cared. I had no grooming standard but my own to uphold, and that was a pretty loose proposition, at least when I was alone. But lately, I had to admit, I'd been feeling an irritating pressure to adopt some socially approved image of proper womanhood, which often involves careful selection of flattering clothes, cosmetics, and frequent visits to the hair salon. I'm all for enhancing and adorning, but at what point does enhancement become cover, mask, make-up: self-exile, self-vanishing? In a culture that generally values fleeting youth and beauty beyond all other facets of a woman, where is solid ground, the bedrock, beneath her feet?

I walked an uncertain path between a youthful wildness that attracts its own unearned attention and the less-sanctioned appeal of a woman at a certain age, gone a little too wild. In a world where people are dying of starvation and epidemic disease, aging is an admirable event. But the educated West is alarmingly short on perspective and reason, and I was dismayed as any aging starlet at the palpable attention my mere physical presence no longer engendered.

Of course I was also dismayed that I even noticed.

When the sun splintered the foggy gray clouds, I stuffed the sleeping bag and took down the tent. Flipper rolled on his back, sawed his legs in the air, waited without shame for me to rub his old belly. Emmy lifted her ears and nose and growled softly at some disturbance only she could sense. "It's okay," I told her. "No barking." She looked off into the distance and back at me, then came to lean against my legs. She stood patiently while I fastened her saddlebags. She had learned backpacking since yesterday, and she already trusted me in this as in everything else.

I heaved my own load onto my back. One shoulder winced against the weight. An ankle rolled on a loose rock.

I'd planned to hike up to the pass with its view of the "backside" of the southern Teton Range, but there were still deep and slick snowfields above me. I'd seen the view before, and would, no doubt, again, but today I wasn't particularly seeking the big-vista experience.

I slipped down the trail, stubbing toes and wobbling under the weight of pack and gravity. It occurred to me that if I spaced out I might crash, so I gave my attention to a walking meditation, saying aloud, "I am walking. I know that I am walking." This kept my attention on legs and feet and trail for a while, but eventually the refrain became silent, then a song in my head, to the tune of "when you're smiling, when you're smiling, the whole world smiles with you."

But I knew the mountains could roll me, toss me, bury me without apology or guilt.

Even so, I navigated without crashing, just occasional trips and stumbles to keep me alert. Flipper and Emmy still sat down on the trail and gave me mournful looks even though all the dog food was gone and their packs weighed hardly anything. But they didn't fool me. I knew they were the happiness that pads willingly beside me, that shadows me to tent or house, follows me anywhere without question.

They would follow me into Grand Teton National Park, on the other side of these limestone mountains, but dogs are not welcome there. The park boundary line includes the dramatic granite peaks of the Tetons and much of the charismatic megafauna—the big, heartstoppingly beautiful symbols of the wild. The less startling side, where I hiked, had been excluded from the park, though it was part of the same range of mountains. Without the glamour of National Park designation, the windward slope of the Tetons drew far fewer visitors.

Like anyone's, my eyes have been seduced by photogenic phenomena of nature: national parks, large wild creatures, wildly beautiful—and usually young—people. But I wonder if such focus on the obviously grand conditions us to disregard the less visually arresting: closer vistas, small animals, indistinct birds, fleeting wildflowers, worn faces of elders. The grand vista or visage doesn't need close scrutiny to be appreciated: one look is overwhelming. So overwhelming we might mistakenly imagine we know all there is to know about such a place or face.

An icon of American beauty, Marilyn Monroe, once said, "I want to grow old without face-lifts. They take the life out of a face, the character. I want to have the courage to be loyal to the face I've made." But Marilyn self-vanished, and who knows if one legendary woman's loyalty to her aging self might have enlarged what the cultural eye regards as worthy of celebration.

A reasonable person knows that age means *more*, not less. At least the mind knows this. But how many carry the confidence of years gracefully, without apology or regret?

It was their siren call I strained to hear, above the clamor of glamour culture.

In sun-parched meadows, wildflowers were drying out already, clattering in the slight wind. I stopped to take off my shirt, then hefted the pack again. I walked on, sweaty, dusty, uncombed, wearing dirty blue shorts, a black sport top. The sun burned my bare abdomen like a lover's hand.

I wandered around pale boulders the size of trucks, splattered with rust and black lichen. I picked up the fragment of a bivalve shell, its interior cemented with sand-turned-to-stone.

In the ancient sediment and lichen I recognized bones and flesh. Earth's body in formidable age: eroded, pitted with sinkholes, scarred with fossils, whiskered with algae and fungus. Experienced rock. Stone that had been around. Articulate with stories of the epochs.

My skin was already wrinkled as tissue paper, cracked as desert mud, porous and mottled as the fissured limestone. I bore scars of burns, cuts, scrapes, thorn-lashings, collisions with rocks and asphalt, too much sun. Fingers had begun to twist like old whitebark pine. My history. My own fossils. Stories written on the body, the only book I will carry everywhere until I die.

In the wild land of big mountains and rivers, I was not the cultural deviant I might have become in the land of tidy suburbs or skyscrapers. In my chosen homeland, there were women who, at sixty, seventy, and even eighty years old, backpacked, canoed, skied, and climbed: a wild tribe, still breaking trail.

My friend Dodie Stearns, at eighty, spent each summer living "off the grid" and canoeing in far northern Canada, then skied all winter at Jackson Hole. Months away from "civilization" each year offers a particular intimacy with wild creatures: once Dodie squatted to pee in the woods and looked up in time to see a white wolf examining her with curiosity.

Another legendary inspiration, Lorraine Bonney, then age sixty, ran the Colorado River with me at historic high water. On a nine-week sea kayak trip in Alaska's Prince William Sound, Lorraine touched a humpback whale as it rose under her boat. Well into the AARP years, Lorraine worked in Antarctica and traveled to Everest base camp on a trash-removing expedition. Her backcountry grooming ritual included trimming her hair with the tiny scissors on her Swiss Army knife.

In 1924, Mardy Murie honeymooned by dogsled up Alaska's Koyukuk River with wildlife biologist Olaus Murie, with whom she worked passionately on behalf of wilderness. When I told Mardy—who, with Olaus, was largely responsible for establishing the Arctic National Wildlife Refuge—that she was one of my heroes, she said, "Why? All I did was follow that man." But in 1998, thirty-five years after Olaus had died, Mardy received the Presidential Medal of Freedom for a life dedicated to conservation. She was then nearly ninety-six years old.

Once, upon returning from backpacking in the Beartooth Mountains, I ran into Mardy's dear friend Inger Koedt, who'd also just come home from backpacking. When I asked where she'd been, she named a lake high in the Tetons, far from any established trail. Inger reported that her trip had been altogether fine except that in one particularly exposed spot she had asked her son to rope her up for safety. Inger was past eighty at the time.

These were ordinary women, women who'd navigated careers, children, husbands, and more than the requisite tragedies, women whose imaginations had not atrophied along with their ovaries, physically and soulfully manifested women who'd left only a scattering of humble markers on their paths. Ordinary as limestone, ordinary as diamonds.

Naturally, the young clerks at the mountaineering shop were not the only ones who ignored them, but this wild tribe had broken trail without fanfare for so long they were way beyond caring, way beyond even noticing.

They were women who had found home in their bodies, home in relationship to the body of Earth. Bedrock.

I was not yet as socially aberrant as women whose idea of a senior moment might be an ascent of the Grand Teton, a multiweek river trip in the outback, or testifying before the U.S. Congress, but if I were fortunate, I would learn to track their footsteps, follow their deviant, white-haired trail.

Two people ascended the switchbacks, breathing hard under the weight on their backs. I could see them below me, through the trees.

"Did you remember the water filter?" a woman's voice asked.

"Ben loaned me his," the other replied.

"How far is it?"

"I forgot the map."

Rounding the bend, the young women came into view. I stepped aside to let them pass. "Hello," I said.

"Hey, how's it going?" they gasped in unison, both faces flushed with exertion.

"It's the best," I said, calmed by shade, descent, and an overnight approach toward my own bedrock.

The hikers stopped beside me on the trail. Emmy and Flipper leaned against the women's legs, pushed their furry heads into the women's hands. "There are so many wildflowers," one woman said. "We're trying to learn them."

"Are you alone?" the other asked, rubbing Emmy's head and looking at me.

I nodded. "Except for the dogs."

"Cool," she said. "It's our first backpacking trip without our boyfriends."

"Hey," the other one said. "Do you know wildflowers? There was one growing in the boggy areas down the trail that we couldn't find in the field guide. Kind of purple, and short?"

"Self-heal," I said in an inexplicable outburst of memory before I whistled Flipper and Emmy down the trail.

Solo Celebration

MARY LOOMIS

I STOP CLIMBING AT DUSK, EXHAUSTED and hungry. My whole body feels swollen and sore: a combination of dehydration, strenuous work, and exposure to the strong, relentless sun. The dirty residue from ropes running over carabiners has stained my hands black and I am sticky from the cooled sweat on my body. Never mind the grime, all I want is to eat and drink. It doesn't take long to find dinner: a can of ravioli, and a large piece of cake wrapped in aluminum foil, at the top of the haul bag. I pull out my knife, cut open the lid, and sink back onto the cool, granite wall with a mouthful of cold pasta and processed meat.

Somewhere between dessert and Kool-Aid the alpine-glow fades away and surges into a sunset of purple and blue. Car headlights snake in a bright white line along the Valley floor and then disappear into the Wawona Tunnel.

I still remember the first time I came to Yosemite Valley. It must have been around the end of May since we had just celebrated my birthday. Mom, Dad, and I drove up from the San Franciso Bay in our yellow minivan for the long weekend. They even let me invite my best friend, Sabine, along. Besides me, she was the only girl in the whole third grade who played baseball and football with the boys at recess instead of swinging on the monkey bars with the rest of the girls. We had matching frog shorts and liked to wear our hair in braids. I remember we

45

rounded a bend in the road and drove into a tunnel, the same one I am looking at now. When we popped through on the other side, an enormous, smooth rock wall filled the sky: Half Dome. I had to lean my head back to take it in. Maybe my memory has been exaggerated by time; I was only nine. But regardless, I was spellbound. It was the first time I felt the beauty of the natural world throw me without hesitation, warning, or choice into the magic of experiencing total awe.

I have climbed Half Dome several times since that first trip years ago and by chance it has always been at defining moments in my life; times when I was taking a definite step toward a lifestyle, a community, and a profession that I never intentionally planned on being a part of but somehow, consciously or not, let happen. Blame it on serendipity or something of the sort; here I am back on Half Dome, this time to rope-solo a big-wall aid route for the first time.

I arrived in Camp Four just a few days ago. My work commitments, guiding out in the Rockies, didn't start until the beginning of June, still two weeks way. Desert climbing was getting too hot for my taste, the mountains still too iffy, and so I decided to come here. It felt impulsive; I didn't have a climbing partner, and Yosemite, en route as I was from Utah to Colorado, was entirely out of the way. But the minute I decided to start driving west, it felt right.

Rope-soloing an aid route doesn't feel to me as crazy as it might sound. Once I decided to try the route alone, I realized I was not surprised or overwhelmed by the plan. I think subconsciously I've been planning an undertaking like this all along. Ten years ago, back when I was eighteen and had just started climbing I defined this climb as the ultimate test of competency and confidence. A multiday climb thousands of feet off the ground doesn't allow for much margin of error, even with a partner. Alone, that same climb takes on a whole new level of seriousness and intensity; there is only one person around to deal with potential risks and hazards. There is no one else up on the wall to use as a resource for answers or to rely upon for companionship, share the hard work, or help if something goes wrong. Even if I never end up actually needing those things on a route, in the back of my mind I know they are always there ready and waiting, part of the all-inclusive package that comes with a good climbing partner. If the route does not go well, I have no one to blame but myself, and the consequences could be severe. The impossibility of the idea, borne from the perspective of a new climber, turned into a challenge that has long pushed me and finally brought me back in a full circle to this place I am in right now; this place where finally I actually have the skills, grown from long alpine routes, expeditions, and other walls, to safely undertake this endeavor. I wouldn't do it if I didn't feel ready.

I put the remains of dinner away, slide into my sleeping bag, and try to position myself for a comfortable night's sleep. I negotiate the long daisy chain running off my harness like an umbilical cord, attached with a carabiner to the sturdy anchor upon which my small universe hangs. I pretend to study the xeroxed Half Dome topo but I am too tired. I fold up the worn copy and turn off my light.

Although the Valley floor is already baking in sunshine (one of the downfalls of a north-facing route), I wake up in a shadow and I keep my hat and warm jacket on until I am done with breakfast and the haul bag is packed. I can hear the muffled voices of climbers below me on a trail and the familiar clink of carabiners and hardware hitting one another in an irregular staccato beat. I peel off layers, knowing that once I start moving I will be warm. The gear sling, thrown around my shoulders, is an awkward addition of fifty pounds of metal to my 140-pound frame; seventeen cams, twenty-three nuts, four hexes, six tricams, sixty non-locking carabiners, fifteen lockers, plus a pile of webbing and two sixty-meter ropes. I am reminded of the comparison John Sherman, bouldering guru, made between different outlets of sex and climbing. Bouldering, like the art of sensual massage, is pure and minimalist in nature. Aid climbing, weighted down by endless amounts of gear, ropes, and accessories, is more like sadomasochism and bondage. I couldn't agree more. I have ballooned to almost two hundred pounds. What I would do for just a pair of slippers and my chalk bag! I tie in and get to work sliding a number-two nut into place.

With no one to swap out on the sharp end, I lead every pitch. It is a long and tedious task.[1] But I enjoy the intense focus and the slow, monotonous rhythm. I pull a small TCU from the rack and reach high for a placement; nope, too small. I try again with a larger one. I test the placement's strength and reach down for the lead rope. I feel relaxed inside. Today I am climbing with less hesitation. Yesterday, I felt awkward, sometimes reluctant to trust my pieces and high step in spots where normally I wouldn't hesitate. I was double- and triple-checking knots, systems, and gear. I don't have a partner up here to routinely check me as we always do. I am the one who has to make sure that my carabiner is locked, that I am unclipping the correct line, and that I feel confident the anchor will hold. Although attention to detail is more crucial than ever when climbing alone, climbing in a tense and worried state can be just as hazardous. I try hard not to let it happen, but sometimes my imagination slips away and what-ifs run through my mind.

Climbing has always been as much a mental as a physical undertaking for me. The memory of a past fatal accident still haunts me and can interrupt my concentration without warning, starting me on the destructive cycle of second-guessing myself. Toward the end of yesterday I started doubting my pro placements and pictured myself falling, pieces pulling out one by one all the way back to the anchor. When I start down that slippery slide, the focus, calm, and concentration needed to climb strong and safe is lost. Like most things it is a matter of time. Now, with a handful of pitches under my belt, I am moving toward a healthier balance.

I pass three guys at the belay on the top of the twelfth. I try to snuff out the little flicker of pride I feel sneaking in. But undoubtedly I will see these guys again at some point, they will pass me, and the hierarchy my ego is creating will be established all over again.

At the top of the fourteenth pitch I rest. I am annoyed and tired after spending a frustrating forty-five minutes dealing with a haul bag and a chimney. The most I can look forward to is yet another chimney on the next pitch. I am losing steam and motivation. Friends warned me about this route, infamous for eating haul bags along the way. But my core of eternal optimism (or stubbornness, some would say) failed to listen. Screw the bravado; doing a job intended for two with only one is a pain in the ass. I am slowing down. I need a break, some food, and water. I planned on getting to the top of the seventeenth pitch today, Big Sandy Ledge. I wipe my face on my shirtsleeve, leaving a long, dark stain of sweat and dust. I look like a banker gone awry—my white button-down shirt, the best thing around for keeping off the sun, and my sturdy brown khakis, tattered and covered with the dirty remnants and scars of climbing.

I pull a new water jug out of the haul bag and try to pace myself but gulp the entire bottle, hardly stopping to breathe. I sit full and bloated, trying to let the water settle. I think back to the first time I climbed "The Dome"—twelve years old, my first backpacking trip ever. I begged Mom for a pair of hiking boots but she accused that this, like the tennis racket she'd bought the summer before, was just a fad. So up the Cable Route I went in my slippery, old white Nikes, fighting the fear I might slide off, gripping the thick cable handrails as tightly as I could, too focused on each step to even savor the view. Step by step, just as I am doing now. Years later, I returned for an overnight on top of the Dome. It was the grand finale to a long trans-Sierra route. I was sixteen. Our hiking party arrived at the top of the cables just as the sun started setting. It was a moment so full of beauty and happiness. For a fleeting moment everything was perfect. We raced around taking pictures, posing as silhouettes against the sunset. I remember watching, with curiosity and amazement, a few climbers pop over the edge of the summit plateau, silent and smeared with dirt, big cylindrical bags on their backs. They continued toward the descent despite the dark, models of endurance and athleticism. Four years later during my first summer working as a guide, I made the trip from car up to the summit and back in a day, all in time for a round of beers at the bar that night. I felt so grown-up and tough, glowing with a smug smile. Here I am all over again for another first.

When my stomach finally settles, it is time to move on. I jug the fifteenth pitch, thankful it is only a breeze that cools me instead of a strong wind that could twist my ropes like tangled kite lines. So far, as the forecast predicted, the weather has been perfect—sunny California skies with warm spring temps. My thoughts drift to the first wall I aided a few years ago in Zion. I figured aiding was an important skill for any climber, but really more than anything I just wanted to spend the night on a portaledge. The climb went well. We topped out on Halloween dog-tired and happy. Wise friends cautioned that my first big wall inevitably would feel like a punishment; sadomasochism and bondage at its best. But I ended up loving it; the slow and methodical process of aid leading, the delicate balancing act of stepping up in the etriers, the upward glide of ascending when the rhythm is right, and more than anything, the amount of uninterrupted time spent on the rock. So often it is the sheer size of a wall that leaves us speechless and is forever remembered. Rarely is the micro of the grand macro examined: all the different grains, crystals, and how their colors change in the shifting light, the ancient green, yellow, black, and brown lichens clinging for life to the steepest of angles, tiny plants with delicate, dainty flowers that belie the brute strength needed to claw their way into tiny rock seams and thrive, and all the feelings of granite—hot, cold, polished, and rough, against bare skin. For small chunks of time, like this, I am close enough to listen, see, smell the rock's secrets.

By six o'clock I am still one pitch away from Big Sandy Ledge. I fight the frustration swelling inside. I want to climb faster; I know I can climb faster. Instead I force myself to stop until the rushed, frustrated feeling passes. Who am I climbing faster for? Apart from myself, no one up here could care less when I finish.

I share the belay ledge that night with two small parties of guys. We make small talk about where we are from and other objectives in the Valley. They quiz me: Where do I live? Wyoming. What do I do? Teach and guide. Is it true there is no open-container law in Wyoming? I can't remember. And where the hell is my boyfriend? A question I don't even bother answering.

But I bow out of the small talk early and worm my way into my sleeping bag. My body feels like a limp sponge, every ounce of energy wrung out to dry. I want to get an early start in the morning. The route's prime pitches, the "Zigzags," start off right above my head.

I end up sleeping later than intended. My watch is missing from my neck. Instead, I find it wrapped around my socks at the bottom of the sleeping bag. By the time I make my way out of bed, two of the guys, who obviously heard their alarms, have almost completed the first pitch of the Zigzags.

It is the third and final section of the Zigzags when I hear a call from below politely asking to pass. It is the other party from the ledge, done with their cold coffee, bagels, and already on my tail. I call down an invitation to come on up, feeling a little sheepish that they are passing me but understanding and knowing full well that I'd do the same in a similar situation. They pass by with words of encouragement and promises of a celebration that night at their spot in Camp Four.

I am one pitch away from the top. I push myself to stay on task and focus. Hurrying will not help me but steady efficiency will. I do not want to spend another night up here. I do not want to deal with the dark. I am tired and ready to be done. I have a way to go yet; descending the cables, the rocky steps of Quarter Dome, and a steep eight-mile trail back to the car all await me. Although I am only halfway done, I am ready for the climbing to be over. By now this experience is all about the destination. I want to turn my brain off, disengage from the intense focus, decision-making, concentration, and just sit with a pint of ice cream and beer.

Finally, I top out on lead. I am on the summit. A wave of ease and relief spills through me. Suddenly the urgency of arrival evaporates. I am reenergized with a fifth or maybe sixth wind. I grant myself a moment to look around at the Valley below and feel ecstatic. More slowly than usual, I build an anchor and rappel back down to clean and rig the haul bags one last time, focusing not so much on each precise step but the bigger picture—how each step has cumulated to bit by bit bring me closer to the close of a successful and safe climb, closer to the summit I've sought. I want to savor my ending.

By the time I have cleaned and hauled, officially safe and sound on top and done with the climb, Half Dome's summit plateau is empty. There is no one left to ask me what I just did or congratulate me. No one looks over in awe as I did that night up here so many years ago. The high I'm riding inside takes a nosedive. Disappointment hits. For the first time since I started this climb I am lonely. But, just like the climb, this is my celebration to make or break. If I've had the strength and tenacity to get up this thing alone I sure as hell have it in me to make up a suitable celebration of my own. Euphoria returns; waves of warmth flood through me. I walk around in long, exaggerated strides stretching out my legs, and I feel weightless. Roving marmots scurry back into the rocks. It feels so good to no longer be hanging. The valley is bathed in a golden and pink haze that grows darker by the second. The cars are still down there snaking in a bright white line toward Wawona Tunnel. I feel all alight inside. I can't stop smiling; it's another one of those perfect moments. I shake my sweaty mess of hair free from my helmet and direct a victory cry to the sky. There is no one around to hear me and it feels just right that way.

[1] Essentially, I am climbing every section of the route twice. I attach one end of the rope to the anchor while I tie the rope's top end into my harness. Then, I grab a bite of rope from the end that is fixed to the anchor and clove-hitch myself into the rope about eight feet away from the anchor. I place a piece of protection as high as I can safely reach. I reach up and clip my left etrier into the piece of protection with a new carabiner. I reach up again and do the same with my right etrier. I slowly ascend the webbing staircase my etriers make until I am high as I can go. I set my Fifi hook, a small metal hook girth hitched to my harness with a short leash, onto my etrier at whatever height I have stopped. I can now sit down, hanging securely off the Fifi, with my hands free. I reach down and adjust the clove hitch, giving myself enough slack to clip the rope onto another carabiner on the newly placed protection above, but careful to keep enough tension so that the rope would pull taunt in case of a fall. (There are now three carabiners on the placed piece.) I have officially moved up a piece. I get to work on placing the next piece of pro. I then reach back for my spare etrier and reach up to clip it into the new piece of pro. The cycle of placing pro, clipping in, stepping up in my etriers, continues until I reach the next anchor. Once there, I attach the rope I climb on and the haul rope I trail behind to the anchor. I rappel down, cleaning protection out of the route as I go. I rig the haul bag to the rope, set it loose from the bottom anchor, and disassemble the bottom anchor. Now I ascend the rope with mechanical ascenders. Back up top I will then have to haul the haul bag, via a pulley system, up to the new anchor. Once I am done the process starts all over again.

Turning Back

SHERRY SIMPSON

A t FIRST I THOUGHT OF THE HIKE along the old Circle-Fairbanks Trail as a walking meditation. For at least a week, maybe more, I would walk with only my blue heeler Jenny for company. I would spend all day, every day, quiet with my thoughts. For fifty-eight miles I would hike through heat and rain and mosquitoes on a hilly route I didn't know. On the other end, seven or eight days away, my husband would greet someone different from the person he left at the trailhead. Of this I was sure.

For weeks I practiced with map and compass. I bought a GPS and learned to use it. I did girls' pushups twenty at a time. I filled my pack with the heaviest items—tent, sleeping bag, pad, clothes, stove, fuel, water filter—and marched along the first two miles of the trail to remind my feet and back of the task ahead. At the path's high points, I looked across the domes, still patchy with snow, and imagined myself walking toward the horizon, soon.

I told all of my friends about the trip. It was a way of not chickening out. Some of them told me stories, just as mothers can't help but describe the pains of childbirth to pregnant women. One friend said, "I feel I should say that the worst mosquitoes I've ever encountered were on the Circle-Fairbanks Trail." Another described following the footprints of a solo hiker near the White River in the St. Elias Mountains until the footprints disappeared into the river, which is what happened

53

to the hiker: he disappeared into the river after trying to float it in a small raft.

I could not help myself; I looked up news stories about him and about other solo hikers, too. There was the thirty-six-year-old man who vanished in Glacier Bay National Park, leaving behind his tent, food, and most of his gear. The rangers decided he "strolled away from his camp, got lost, suffered hypothermia, and in his confusion fell into the water or crawled out of sight beneath a rock." What they meant was: "We have no idea what happened to him." There was the young woman who lost her way during a bird-watching day hike on one of the most popular trails near Fairbanks. Three days later, searchers found her but not her little dog, which had wandered off into the woods, to be eaten by bears or eagles or who knows what.

This was not the first time I would be alone out in the woods somewhere, but it was the first time I would hike such a distance by myself, relying on my own judgment, strength, skills. I would have to be brave. That's why I wanted to do it, I suppose. At home I am the sort of person who is afraid to answer a ringing phone because a stranger might ask for something that can't be refused, such as a donation to a suspiciously obscure charity or a subscription to a magazine I don't want. I spend long moments each day worrying about things that can't be changed, such as what I should have told the person on the phone instead of "yes." I vex myself with long, imaginative dramas about things that haven't happened but could: falling elevators, mysterious diseases, wrongful criminal accusations. To a person who frets her way through daily life, it comes as a relief to lie awake nights and think through real problems: getting lost, falling ill, dying alone in some ravine.

Other, less definable worries occupied me, including how to keep a clear head no matter what. Never mind about losing the way—what about losing *it*, the all-important sense of calm and control that must be kept intact? Now and then I would stir restlessly and reach my hand toward my sleeping husband, trying to soothe that jumpy feeling deep in my chest. It was a familiar sensation, the fear of being afraid, of being so swamped by uncertainty and dread that I wouldn't know what to do. It was a feeling that had texture, dimension, weight.

The night before I left, I gathered the gear scattered about my living room and stuffed it into my big blue pack. When I hefted the load onto my back, I pitched backward a step, then forward, struggling to remain upright. My husband laughed. I took everything out and ditched whatever seemed excessive: extra bandages, a minidisc recorder, rope. The pack lightened by perhaps nine or ten ounces. Surely this was the heaviest weight I had ever borne.

I did not know what else to leave behind. One person has to carry everything.

Scott drove me to the trailhead on a cool June morning. We climbed toward Cleary Summit on the Steese Highway, then turned onto bumpy dirt roads and ricketed toward the trailhead. Jenny paced back and forth across the back seat, smearing the windows with her muzzle. She is a dog who lives in constant anticipation. The radio repeated a news item about a thirty-year-old Alaskan killed the previous day when his truck rolled over. He had been a top athlete and a two-time competitor in the winter Wilderness Classic, an arduous 125-mile race through the Wrangell Mountains. Any day of the week, a person could die. A person doesn't have to slip down a mountainside, or get mauled by a bear, or disappear into the wilds to die. A person could drive to work and be killed, just like that.

Mosquitoes hummed in a thick fog at the trailhead. I grunted as I struggled into the pack and buckled myself to it. Scott attached a tinny bell to Jenny's collar, not to alert bears but to help me keep track of her. He sprayed me front and back with bug dope. He photographed us standing by the sign that said "Circle-Fairbanks Historical Trail," and the traitorous part of my brain wondered if that would be the picture they'd put in the paper once the search started. Scott had never once tried to dissuade me from this hike; he just assumed I knew what I was doing. He held my face and kissed me goodbye. "Be careful," he said, and I nodded mutely and turned up the trail. The next time I looked, he was driving away, and Jenny and I had no choice but to keep going.

The clouds evaporated as the day heated, and the mosquitoes dropped away in the sun. The pack's straps rasped against my collarbone, and a miasma of bug dope rolled off me. I leaned against a rocky slope and gulped water, letting it slop down my throat and chest. I offered Jenny a slurp and glanced at my watch. We had been walking for thirteen minutes. Twenty minutes later, I trudged up a small slope to a rock outcropping, marked by beer cans and cigarette butts as a scenic overlook. Posts indicated each passing mile, but I hadn't seen the first marker yet. I was terribly afraid we hadn't reached it yet, because if it were going to take me an hour to walk a mile, then I might not get home before the end of summer.

A breeze stirred the creamy, simple blooms of grass of Parnassus around our feet. "Thirsty?" I asked Jenny. She wagged her stub. A ridiculous tail for a dog. "Your tail is ridiculous," I told her. I could see I would be spending a lot of time talking to my dog. I missed Scott already. I heaved off the pack and poured water into Jenny's fold-up bowl. Then I sat on pointy rocks and drank deep draughts still cold from my kitchen faucet. Finding water would be a problem out here, but I could not stop gulping.

The hills roller-coastered around us. New leaves of aspens and birches riffled in the slow sea of air. A massive hard-rock gold mine named Fort Knox ground away in the distance, hidden from view. It was the newest quarry in a country that had been mined top to bottom for a hundred years. The maps are strewn with tiny Xs, hash marks, and crossed picks that symbolize prospects, mines, and tailings on every creek. Around here entire gold-rush towns have long since eased back into the brush, leaving only names: Cleary, Gilmore, Golden City, Olnes. Pictures of Dome City, not far from the trailhead, show a thriving community built by former luminaries of the Klondike. The town included three banks, police and fire departments, a mayor, a stage company, and plenty of hotels and bars. Today—nothing.

The Circle-Fairbanks Trail is a narrow four-wheel drive road at the start, muddy and rutted with tracks from all-terrain vehicles, motorcycles, horses, moose, wolves, and bears. It is said the Athabascans originally used it, or some version of it, as a hunting and trade route. Then prospectors wandered through, frisking the creeks for gold. When diggings proved rich, lots of people suddenly had reason to travel from Circle City on the Yukon River into the Birch Creek region. When a scruffy Italian prospector named Felix Pedro panned colors from a creek not far from this dome, hopeful people poured in from the Yukon and the Chandalar country to a new gold camp named Fairbanks.

Mail, cattle, sheep, passengers, and supplies crossed the country between Circle City and Fairbanks. So much gold traversed this route that the "Blue Parka Bandit" shadowed the trail, politely but firmly robbing stages and lone miners of their fortunes. In 1928, the Steese Highway borrowed some of the trail, and then there wasn't much reason to use the rest. Most of the roadhouses closed, and the route lapsed, used only by dog mushers, snowmachiners, hikers, horse riders, and off-road riders. A few stubborn miners drive the trail to their claims, but the rest of us use it for fun.

I rolled my pack over and loosened the shoulder cinches. In a process that seemed to grow harder each time rather than easier, I hoisted it to one bent knee, wormed my right arm through the strap, twisted my left arm behind my back, and, stooping over, tugged it onto my back. Involuntary sounds emerged from my mouth that I thought I wouldn't be making for another twenty or thirty years. "Mother of God, why is this pack so heavy?" I groaned. Jenny stared at me, ears perked, pink tongue dangling wetly. "Why aren't you wearing a pack?" I asked. "You could at least carry your own food."

Recently I'd begun to wonder if her sharp eyes—eyes that could spot a bread crumb falling onto the floor from ten feet away—had clouded a little. Sometimes I had to clap my hands to catch her attention. Her muzzle had whitened, and she no longer made wild, acrobatic leaps to catch Frisbees. In dog years she was ninety-one. Bringing her along seemed a bit like dragging your grandmother on the Appalachian Trail. Nevertheless, I had assumed Jenny would like walking with me, and of course, she did. What a grand creature a dog is.

Until now, I hadn't given much thought to the actual hiking. Mostly I'd concentrated on simply getting here. Several months earlier I had spent three days in the hospital when outpatient surgery had unexpectedly become inpatient surgery. For a time, the diagnosis had been vague, and alarming words had been bandied about—growth and malignant and so on. I'd signed papers authorizing the removal of any suspicious tissue, up to and including entire reproductive organs—not that the doctor expected such a thing, he kept saying. During the procedure, the surgeons discovered I was suffering from endometriosis, a fairly common problem in which uterine tissue colonizes new territory, but they had been forced to abandon the minor procedure of a laparoscopy, with its modest nick through the bellybutton, and instead had slit open my lower abdomen and mucked about in my internal organs, leaving me with a six-inch scar and a sore belly.

I had shared the hospital room with an eighty-year-old woman who'd had an abdominal tumor the size of a basketball removed, a tumor she hadn't known was there until she'd undergone a scan for back problems. She was proud of a Polaroid documenting her remarkable tumor, a photograph I repeatedly fended off. My doctor, though, ambushed me in the follow-up exam with Technicolor pictures of my body cavity with organs splayed out during surgery. I wasn't sure which was worse: actually seeing my own innards, or knowing that total strangers had been photographing them while I was as insensible as I ever hope to be this side of death.

I spent a good part of the spring huffing at crunches, scratching the red scar that embossed my belly, trying to regain a feeling of wholeness and strength. This hike would prove my health, my vigor, my endurance. Still I couldn't seem to shake the red truth of that photograph.

I sang. It seemed early in the trip to holler spirit-bolstering songs, but I sang anyway. I stepped among the tracks of all who had passed recently—horses, people, wolves, a moose, and her newborn calf—and I sang lullabies and hymns, love songs, and ditties composed entirely of nonsense. Jenny paced and panted just behind me. Usually she insisted on leading any expedition. When she was younger, it drove her to distraction on berry-picking expeditions if any of us wandered about; she spent all her energy trying to herd us into one safe, compact group. Today the heat seemed to have dulled her usual energy, and she lagged. Whenever we paused, she flopped in the dirt and waited, eyes half-closed.

Jenny didn't like me when we first got her as a repo dog, thirteen years before. Scott's boss had bred Queensland heelers, also known as Australian cattle dogs, and he had retrieved Jenny from her new owners when he discovered that the puppy was living night and day in a garage lined with Visqueen on the floor. He next sold her to a man who had never asked his wife if she wanted a dog. She didn't. A week later, I was visiting Scott at work when the embarrassed man returned with a gray-and-red puppy that rocketed around at near the speed of light, ears flattened, tongue curled. We took her home.

She was four months old and had missed crucial time being socialized. She bared her teeth and rolled her eyes suspiciously whenever I tried to pet her, no matter how much I complimented her fine markings, the black that circled her eyes like kohl and tipped her ears, the silvery sheen of her coat and her ruddy belly, the white streak on her fawn-colored face. Within a few days, she decided to be my dog after all, a job she took far too seriously. It was years before she would let other people in the house without terrifying them, though once she did warn me about a man I was too stupid to realize was dangerous. Most of her attitude problems I attributed to chronic underemployment. Lacking cows to organize, she bossed around our two cats and the other dog, a male husky-Lab who was much larger than she was but who had an IQ less than his body weight. Jenny had not only brains but opinions she couldn't keep to herself. We called her piercing yap the "Vulcan Death Bark."

Unfortunately, she did not see me as the alpha female so much as an outsized littermate who occasionally made irritating demands and wasn't particularly accommodating about sharing the bed. But everywhere I went, she followed, even from room to room in the house. "Mind your own beeswax," I chided her one day, and Scott said, "But you are her beeswax." Out here, it was comforting being somebody's beeswax.

At every milepost I stopped and entered the position in my GPS. It tracked my progress, though the pencil ticks on the map and the satellite readings told me nothing my feet and back didn't know already. Mile two, uphill on a wooded slope. Mile three, along a forested straightaway, passing a leghold trap on the trail. Mile four, curving upward against the outside of a dome, where a runnel of clear water dribbled from the thawing tundra. Mile five, alongside two fresh sets of bear tracks pressed into the mud.

We passed an explosion of white-gray fur, and I panicked briefly when I saw Jenny nosing a caribou leg near the trail. For all I knew, that pair of bears lurked nearby protecting a kill. A prickly, urgent feeling quickened my steps. I began bellowing love songs. It's my belief that bears like love songs best. The mucky trail turned toward the summit, and so had the bears. I labored on, sweat tracking my face as we rose above the tree line. Just below the dome's crown, where corn snow still lingered, I dropped my pack with an *oof*. For lunch I tired my jaws on jerky as I studied the ranks of black, dense clouds drifting in from the east and searched the tundra for dark shapes nosing through the vegetation. Jenny waited at my feet for the wads of jerky I couldn't conquer. Bear sign didn't alarm her. The possibility that I might not share lunch did.

On the downhill, my left foot slipped and I toppled over in slow motion, gravity pulling the pack onto me. Jenny sniffed at my face pressed against cool mud. I laughed, but this would not do. On my top five list of things I did not want to go wrong: sprains, breaks, or twists of any sort. Pay attention, I scolded myself. Every moment demands attention.

This wasn't all about overcoming fear. I didn't know how else to see the world more clearly than to walk through it. I could not think of a better way to be quiet for a while. True, now that I was here, for long minutes I did not look any higher than my own feet, step by deliberate step up and down those long hills. It was also true that I felt compelled to announce our approach to the wild animals of the country in song and chant, and to speak often to my dog, and to offer a few encouraging words to myself.

But there were these moments, too, when I stopped for no reason that could be named, and stood silently in the middle of the trail, head back, one more person on the way to somewhere that can't be mapped.

A gnarl of thunder followed flashbulb pulses of lightning. Fog and darkness cloaked the distant hills—the hills we headed toward. The only thing I know about lightning is that there's nothing good about being the tallest object on a treeless dome. I walked faster until an upward thrust of shale appeared and offered shelter for the tent. Rain pecked against the fly, and Jenny snorted as she slept, ears twitching whenever thunder ripped close by. The nylon flapped in the wind but the structure held. A few inconstant drips rolled into the dog's water dish, the pot, and the water bottle. All this rain and we'd harvest but a mouthful. I pulled on long johns and rain gear, leaned against the pack and dozed.

At five o'clock, as the storm drifted southward, I screwed the stove together outside the tent while I crouched inside. Flames shot toward my face as I twisted the fuel nozzle the wrong way, and fire lapped at the tent door before I could turn the stove off. My face still warm, I moved the entire setup to a nearby rock and tried again. The pot had just started bubbling when it slipped, spilling stroganoff fixings across the rocks. "This is why we won't sleep where we eat," I told Jenny, who began industriously licking up lumpy sauce and crunchy noodles. So far, a few hours into our trip, I had narrowly avoided twisting my ankle, searing my face, and setting our shelter on fire.

The trail lurched downhill through a boggy black spruce forest until it crossed a dirt track headed toward the Kokomo Creek mine. Jenny waded into a muddy yellow pond to drink and cool off. I dug out a water bag; as dirty as it was, the scummy pond represented the most water we'd seen in four miles.

An empty five-gallon bucket lay beside the trail, and I wondered about bear-baiting stations. Most any bear would run from us with enough warning, but a bear accustomed to slumming around mine camps, digging freebies out of trash cans, and being deliberately attracted by rotting food was exactly the kind of bold bear I feared the most. My thoughts careened now between sore feet and the bear tracks we'd crossed. All I carried was the pepper spray, a small flare for scare value, and an arsenal of Carpenters' songs, which I now grunted, one word per step.

We passed a sign lying in a ditch: "CAUTION. This and all trails are being trapped. Traps and snares in and along trails. Use with caution."

The words "Trap Theives" were lettered within a circle and slash mark. The misspelling made it seem more ominous. Marten sets appeared periodically along the trail, with diagonal poles nailed to a tree, and some shiny trinket—a few inches of tinsel garland, can lids, or even CDs—hanging above the set to mark it.

I revisited my list of top five worries. Perhaps more than injuring myself, I feared that Jenny would get hurt, perhaps by wandering into an abandoned trap or snare. I carried a small first-aid kit jammed with a wire splint, cold pack, gauze and Band-Aids, antibiotic ointments and antiseptic wipes . . . pills for diarrhea, urinary tract infections, runny noses, and miscellaneous aches and pains. But I was not sure I could do anything for an injured dog.

At mile nine, I stopped to set up the tent in a gravelly clearing, proud to have exceeded my daily goal by a mile. It was eight o'clock. A ten-hour day, though filled with stops and interruptions, was nothing to brag about. Jenny snoozed on moss among the trees as I struggled with the tent, which was actually a tarp with a mesh insert for sleeping. Hiking sticks acted as the poles.

I filtered muddy water and filled her dish and my bottle, dosing mine with lemonade crystals to help me choke it down. She licked the dinner pot of leftover rice and beans. She was a terrible chowhound and would do almost anything for food. We had stopped storing cat food cans on the pantry floor when Jenny began shredding them open with her teeth.

I dragged the pack into the bushes but took the pepper spray and signal flare into the tarp. It was hot in there, the black mesh amplifying the sun's rays. A violent hum of mosquitoes and buzz-sawing of wasps enveloped the mesh like a force field. The night would never grow dark, only dim, and for this I was glad. Now and then my mind circled around the game trails emerging from the trees, picturing moose bursting out and trampling the tarp, or a bear moseying into the open, sniffing after my pack, but there was no profit in those thoughts. Every couple of hours I stirred long enough to peer outside. The quiet was liquid, something you'd have to push against to move through. Even the mosquitoes had disappeared. A fine dew misted the tarp and the sleeping bag.

At eight o'clock, the dog and I yawned in each other's faces and then stiffly sat up and stretched. There is a certain kind of earned pain that feels good, that reminds you that your body can almost always do more than you think it can. She looked at the kibble I poured into the pot lid and then looked at me. I sighed and spooned some of my oatmeal with brown sugar and raisins onto her food. Then she ate.

I have a theory that no matter how fast or slow you move in camp, it will always take two hours to pack up and leave. This was true again. At ten o'clock, we took our first tender steps on the trail. Blue sky. No clouds. Not enough water. Already I was hot. And thirsty. I was very thirsty.

Ahead the trail climbed and dropped over the two- and three-thousand-foot hills. Today we'd be hiking hard if we wanted to cover eight miles. I occupied myself thinking up new songs, taking that old chestnut, "Bingo," and improvising to flatter my dog: ". J-E-N-N-Y, J-E-N-N-Y," and so on. I hoped no one would hear. It's the kind of thing saps do with their dogs, such as giving them nicknames, several of them, for any occasion: Jennifer Dogifer, Flufferbutt, Pigger Dog, Doodlebrain, Miss Bossy, and so on. Her ears radared my way as she wondered why I kept calling her when she was standing right there.

So far I hadn't been thinking too many deep and insightful thoughts during my walking meditation. But days and days remained for contemplation, I reminded myself. Plenty of time for spiritual enlightenment. For now, I needed to concentrate on walking as I carried the weight of a third-grader on my back, uphill, in the heat.

As the trail started rising even more steeply, I switched to army chants: "We are climbing up this hill. We will make it yes we will. Won't be the first, won't be the last. We are going to kick its ass. Sound off, one, two, sound off, three, four." I was my own sergeant and recruit, song leader and chorus. Basically, I was doing all the work.

In some ways, traveling with no one but a dog for companionship was ideal. I could stop whenever I wanted. The dinner menu required no polite consultations. Nobody would drop helpful little hints about better ways to erect the tent or build fires. I could pee wherever I wanted. Acting cheerful when I didn't feel cheerful was not required. But a partner who could talk had advantages. It would be nice to say out loud, "Man, this hill is a bitch," and have someone pause and wipe his or her forehead and say, "You can say that again." Jenny looked attentive whenever I spoke out loud, but a person who is complaining needs some validation, some co-complaining. All I could do was order myself onward: "We are getting near the top. When we get there we won't stop."

By noon, only a few mouthfuls of tea-colored water remained in the bottle. I stopped at every trickle, pumped brown sludge from pools gathered in moose tracks as Jenny slurped away. I couldn't afford to be picky; no streams bubbled merrily along the route, no crystalline ponds waited, no rivers rushed by. There were only potholes and a few patches of stale snow in the shadows.

At the next summit, we left the territory of the second topo map and moved onto a third with a smaller scale and less detail. I had already used my compass to correctly divine the proper direction at a confusing fork. Now way-finding depended on the trail itself and a vague, faint pencil sketch that I had transferred from the trail brochure to the map. At the next fork, I studied the rougher uphill path to the left. The thick dashes marking the trail on the wrinkled brochure were dismayingly ambiguous. They could signify either route—over the dome, or just below it. I turned right to continue on the well-used route we had followed successfully so far. It dipped and seemed to round the dome just below the summit rather than crossing over the top.

A fire had swept over these slopes several years back, leaving blackened aspen trunks twisting out of the greenery. I kept on, unease growing as I failed to pass milepost fourteen or fifteen. We stopped for lunch and more water filtering as I studied the map and worried. When the trail dropped downhill abruptly, I stopped and pulled out the GPS, compass, and maps again. "You're not lost if you know where you are," I told myself fiercely. I sighted on the hill below. The trail should head northeast. This route was now clearly trending southeast.

A little while before, I thought I might cry if I discovered we had taken the wrong route. But now I did not feel like crying. I felt tired and mad at myself. Why didn't I pause at that fork to think things through? Why had I been so sure? This was when having a human partner would be good—someone to argue with, to help you think through problems, to blame. But now I had done something stupid, and there was nothing for it but to retrace our steps two miles backward and uphill. There was no one to scold me, either, so I called myself a dumbshit just to make me feel better.

My legs ached as the hill steepened. It was almost four o'clock, and now our mileage lagged behind schedule. After a mile we plodded past a rough mysterious track that jolted upward. I paused to consider. As steep as the path was, I felt certain it headed to the ridge top and intersected the Circle-Fairbanks Trail in a shortcut. I braced my trekking poles in the mud and pushed.

Every few steps, we stopped so I could suck air. The route was not perfectly vertical; it only seemed that way. I mumbled songs to create a rhythm. Hike for a verse, stop. Hike for a verse, stop. Water trickled through ruts. The alders thinned, but I blew my whistle now and then in case bears idled unseen. The sky blackened above the ridge as the daily thunderstorm approached. A solid wind pushed against us as we took the last, struggling steps onto the ridge, where low alpine flowers shuddered. Ahead, the saddle dropped sharply into a spruce-draped valley. Greening hills, hummocky and mottled from cloud shadows, rolled out before us, and the Crazy Mountains surfed in peaks across the horizon. To the left, a bald dome. To the right, an even steeper hill. I strained to see if the lump on top was a cairn, or trail marker. I couldn't tell for sure. Now I regretted leaving the binoculars behind just to save a few ounces.

I dragged the pack behind a rocky bluff and pitched the tarp against the coming rain. Slow down. Think for a little while. Maybe you'll want to eat and push on; maybe you should stay. My feet ached, and the skin joining my big toes to the footpad was raw. Jenny flopped in the lichens and watched me with her head on her paws.

Inside the tent, I fell into the pleasant daze that comes when your feet don't have to move. Every time the wind lifted the tarp's nylon edges, I studied the dome behind us in brief glimpses, searching for a trail. Perhaps there was no obvious route because people could cross the dome's bare flanks any way they pleased. Looking ahead, I imagined faint trails through the lichens and low brush. Tomorrow we'd leave early to make up for wasted miles.

When the wind failed, the mosquitoes rose up, a hidden wave of attackers that had discovered the only warm-blooded creatures for miles. I decided to shift the tarp to face the sun, and rather than walking around to tug out the stakes, I yanked at the taut ropes. A heavy plastic stake snapped from the ground and smacked against my face before I could react. My lip went numb, and blood oozed down my chin. In the compass mirror I studied the welt splitting my lower lip. *Dear Diary: I am one grand adventurer. On Day One I almost set my eyebrows and the tent on fire. On Day Two I took the wrong trail and then belted myself in the face and dripped blood all over the tundra. On Day Three, a bear tracked the scent of blood and ate me up.*

In the tent, Jenny curled at my feet, but every few minutes she sat up and licked at her right hind flank. "Mosquito bites? Poor doggie," I said. My commiseration meant nothing to her. Tomorrow I'd rub a little bug dope over her fur. Tomorrow I'd be much more careful about fire and maps. Tomorrow we'd be in the alpine, high above the world, and well on our way to serenity.

Through the night, her licking became so frantic and compulsive that I woke several times as she shook the tent, jarring loose hundreds of mosquitoes attached to the mesh, intoxicated by the carbon dioxide. I surveyed the tundra each time I woke. A cotton-candy sky rimmed the horizon, and dawn's sparrows lilted in the brush. Low twists of willow and dwarf birch and berry bushes glowed with a faint green haze as spring settled in the alpine.

In the morning, when I sat up, cramped and sore, Jenny was still lapping at her hindquarters. Animals in pain have a glazed, unfocused look; I recognized it in her. She had licked her leg until the fur was sopping, and drool puddled on the tent floor and soaked the sleeping bag. I groaned aloud. "What? What is it?" I asked. Clearly something was wrong, but all she did was eye me and then return to nibbling and licking. She showed me her teeth when I reached toward her leg.

Jenny didn't seem to limp, but she dropped into the soft tundra after we climbed out of the tent and occasionally nosed at her trembling flank. Bugs settled on her nose and on her eyes. In the old days, backcountry travelers simply shot crippled animals and moved on. If she lamed up, I could not possibly carry her to the trail's end, nor could I leave her. I looked out across the hills where green lay upon green, to the southern horizon where the white illuminati of the Alaska Range shimmered in the morning light.

Now that I had to decide whether to turn back, all the reasons for making this trip rose clear and hard before me. One reason was pride, the ego boost of being able to mention casually that once I had hiked by myself for a week, just me and my dog, through the backcountry. I had announced this trip widely. How could I return now having walked only fifteen miles?

Part of it, I admitted, was the hope of encountering some kind of inner peace, maybe even an epiphany, which was the very thing I criticized others for seeking in the wilderness. Probably that was because I desired it so much myself. The last time I had spent a week alone in the woods, fear and loneliness had dropped me to my knees, and then a sense of calm had fallen upon me, as cool and needful as the wind moving through the crowns of ancient trees.

Out here, by myself, I could be honest: Hadn't I made this journey as a way of finding that peace again? After this spring's frightening surgery, didn't I count on some kind of spiritual transformation as a reward for walking a week by myself, for facing my fears? Wasn't I expecting to be struck like a gong sometime along this trail, to vibrate with all the meaning and intensity possible when one climbs a lesser mountain, under a pale sun at midnight, alone? And I had learned nothing so far, except all the foolish things of which I was capable.

But now I did know about something else: the pain of turning back. This was the mildest of journeys, and yet for the first time I understood, a little, why explorers sometimes made such excellent liars. Frederick Cook stood on a minor ridge of Mount McKinley and took the photographs that he hoped would fool the world. He had to. How could he again fail in his quest to summit? Few things are sadder and less interesting than someone who turns back before reaching the top, the pole, the end of the world, or the end of the trail.

Companion and journalist Robert Dunn had mocked Cook's pretensions and airs during their first unsuccessful attempt on Mount

McKinley. But as they crept up the most dangerous slopes, unroped and weak with hunger, he found himself admiring the doctor's steadiness and cursing his own fear. "As for me, is the doing of a thing to be no longer its end, as was in the old adventurous days?" he asked. "The telling of it the end instead?" And here I was, on my little jaunt over well-trod ground, with neither a doing nor a telling to show for it.

Given all that, how much easier to be a prospector than an adventurer. Looking for gold was a solid reason to roam around these hills. But looking for glory, or looking for God—that's just asking for failure.

I melted snow by the potful as I tried to decide what to do. This is your decision now, I thought. Just make it and don't second-guess yourself. Just live with it.

I cried. This is something wilderness is good for: crying as loudly as you want, letting tears and snot run down your face as you shake and sob. I cried because this was not the summer I would walk alone after all. I cried because I hated the idea of retracing my steps. I cried because the shadowed hills ahead would not reveal their mysteries to me.

And I cried because every time I looked at my old dog's face, I could see death in it. I knew she would die some day, of course. We all will. You know it and I know it, but we know it as dispassionately as a memo, as formally as a warranty that we glance at once and then tuck away in a junk drawer we hardly look in. There is no gut truth in such knowledge. But in that moment I knew that my dog would die before long, and soon enough, I will, too. I myself had seen the red and slick tenderness of my own organs. I had seen the future in a lonely old woman holding out a Polaroid of a tumor the size of a basketball.

This, then, was my only discovery: that I had reached the place where middle age tips into loss, when everything worth caring about begins to disappear—not just my beloved dog, but relatives, friends, my husband,

time itself, and all its possibilities. For two days I had walked just to arrive
at this place, just so I could recognize that in life there is no turning back.

I looked at my dog, lying quietly in the tundra, dark eyes fixed upon
me, ears flicking away mosquitoes. There was no dishonor in attending
to her. I thought of all the accounts I'd read of people and dogs in the
North. For every act of indifference or cruelty, there was some old
miner or explorer who valued his dog above any person, any gold. Only
history remembers the husky named Mose, owned by a Klondiker who
told an admirer: "Mister, don't ask me to place a value on my partner. I
couldn't think of it! Why, if I should lose my poke of dust, rather than
to part with Mose, we would hit the trail back and try for another raise."

I could always take this trail again, add my steps to the long proces-
sion of Athabascans, stampeders, freighters, bandits, through-travelers,
all of us collaborating on keeping this passage open across the landscape
and through time. This trail was older than I was, and no doubt would
persist long after my passing. So few people anymore know the country
this way, step by step, hill by hill. Someday I would return. Just not with
my dog, who was moving faster than I toward what awaits us all.

I drank deeply of melted snow from the winter past, and I washed myself
clean with what remained. I collapsed the tarp, and shook out my sleeping bag, and arranged my pack carefully, for we had a long way to travel.
I sat on a rock and inspected my feet and babied my blisters and pulled
my boots back on. I climbed the bluff to sit and memorize the hazy wash
of green in the valleys and the silver gleam of unknown mountains. With
every step I crushed perfect alpine flowers flecking the tundra like con-
fetti.

Jenny followed me, as is her way. For this little while, we were high
above the world, pausing on a path each one of us travels through life.

Then, finally, I tied the bell back onto her collar so I could always find
her, and I hoisted the pack to my shoulders. It had not lightened a bit. I

looked northward once, thinking, *It's not too late to keep on. You've been wrong so many times already. You could take a chance that she'll be all right.*

But even as I turned back, I could feel the sorrow and beauty of the world sinking through me, settling into my flesh, as firm and necessary as the bones that would have to carry me home along this trail.

Reference Points

ELYSE FIELDS

H OME: NO ONE WILL CALL YOU CRAZY if you spend the next twelve hours like other human beings—picking peaches, cursing weather, taking drives. What *is* crazy is putting yourself two hundred feet beneath the Earth so Wind Cave's resource managers can add a few hundredths of a mile to the National Park's official map (a map that already *has* 104 miles, for God's sake). Only, you've been telling the visitors you lead on formal interpretive tours about Jim Pisarowicz, the scientist who descended a hole he'd never seen before on his shoelaces when his rope ran out, about Jan Conn, the explorer who discovered a "spillway" leading to more than seventy miles of new cave—a spillway that had eluded her male counterparts for more than half a century. And visitors have been gaping down the holes on either side of the cave's one and one-quarter miles of paved, lighted trails asking, "Have *you* been to the Lower Level, Ranger?" So for stories' sake, you must exchange your shiny shoes for boots today. You must don a borrowed helmet, strap on knee and elbow pads, turn adventurer.

Elevator Building: Jeremy, a sixteen-year-old kid from the local caving club, *wants* to go surveying. His helmet is on when you arrive, and his cave pack is already snug across his waist. How did he fit his food and water in that compact space? you ask. You are borrowing a slightly bigger pack from the Wind Cave Resource Management stash, and still,

73

your extra headlamp batteries—to say nothing of your emergency long johns—threaten to burst the pack's seams. How did he fit his pee bottle? Wasn't this the first time he'd be in a cave for more than a few hours, too? But Jeremy doesn't have the mind for questions right now. His eyes are luminous and focused on the elevator's silver doors, as if he's made secret contact with the cave shaft on the other side. Feeling uncomfortably solo as you wait for the head of your party, you concentrate on the prairie rain drumming the roof. This is the last time you will experience South Dakota's weather, you realize, for the rest of the day.

Elevator: Here's Jason, the Wind Cave Resource Management intern who is your age but who has, until now, been only a peripheral acquaintance. He has long hair and says "dude" a lot, and he doesn't have the computer-generated maps in order. You don't know whether to feel comforted by the fact that his casual manner might calm you down in the cave or threatened by the fact that his casual manner might get you lost. The combination of the 110-foot drop and the finality of your decision unsettle your stomach. You do not have a man's shoulders for climbing or a caver's natural love for the dark. For all his faith in your fitness, and all his kindness for inviting you along, Jason will not be able to make up for your limitations as an interpretative park ranger down there if you get hurt. This risk is your own.

Lower Landing: The air smells like mold inside this glassed-in antechamber—mold and the cumulated perfume of nicely dressed tour groups. Outside the antechamber, the air is damp and breezy, and smells like nothing. This air belongs to the cave. You walk a hundred yards to the high-vaulted room that marks the first stop on your tour route with visitors. Here is the place where the electric lights get swallowed in holes that look like dragons' mouths, and you tell visitors about Jim and Jan. Jason bends his step to a dwarf-sized hole just off the pavement, one you've certainly passed a thousand times without knowing its significance. He and Jeremy step off the tour route as if its concrete flatness had never existed; you, however, must consciously recalibrate your skeleton for a day of uneven surfaces.

Rome: Jason and Jeremy are too eager and too long-legged to cave at your tour guide's pace. Always you can see one of their boots, but you can't see either caver in his entirety until the three of you stop to breathe on the other side of that first, rugged corridor. Here you find a domed, smooth-polished room dissolved white by the carbonic acid that filled these chambers in the millennia before the water table dropped. "Dude, this is Rome." You squint in the light of your headlamp, still waiting for your eyes to adjust to its limited, orange beam. This is the room where pre–Jan Conn cavers explored hundreds of off-shooting holes only to end up where they started: one of the more cynical of these adventurers, Alvin McDonald, named the room Rome because all roads seemed to lead back to it. You imagine Jan then, wriggling through a low space that others had mistaken as a shadow in the room's corner. Only one out of every ten cavers is a woman. You imagine Jan's single body, her single mind, her single spirit in the narrowest part of a funnel, all on the brink of "spilling" into heretofore unseen sections of the cave. Suddenly, you are glad you came.

Spillway: You're crawling now. The rooms are wide but the ceilings are low. This must be that infamous passage! Only up ahead, the crawlspace narrows even more. Is *that* the spillway? And now it winds left. Is *that* it? By the time you hear the words "Dude! Spillway!" you'd thought you'd passed the landmark long ago. The place you find yourself now looks nothing like the corridor you picture when you narrate Jan's discovery to visitors: It isn't a funnel but rather a slit like the bottom end of a laundry chute. You have to climb up and into it. You realize that the way you picture the cave off-trail in general doesn't exist outside your head.

Frostwork Crawl: You've never seen anything like it. The hall-sized passageway you are moving through is covered with what looks like miniature frosted Christmas trees. These needles of aragonite crystal are identical in composition to the "frostwork" formations you show visitors in the developed parts of the cave. Comparing this frostwork to that frostwork, however, is like comparing the bison that wander the prairie above you to their mammoth predecessors. These Christmas trees are so much bigger, so much more ancient than the crystals you see in your shiny shoes with visitors. Precipitating out of the cave walls through tens of thousands of years, this frostwork was already half-formed when mammoths appeared on Earth. You want to linger, but Jason pushes you on. Because he's been to this part of the cave countless times with Resource Management, it occurs to you, he already has this image in his head—an accurate image of the Frostwork Crawl akin to his accurate image of the spillway—that he can return to at will for bearings and daydreams. At what point, you wonder, will his imagination lose its currency as yours has? Is that the point he printed those maps for? Is that where his sense of adventure begins?

Boxwork Chimney: This was the reason you hesitated this morning. The Lower Level is another hundred feet beneath the corridors you've been traversing and there's only one way down: a two-foot-wide crack in the Earth. When you peer inside the crack, the beam from your headlamp goes down indefinitely. Millimeter-thick calcite plates jut from the inside of the crack at right angles, forming a vertical honeycomb of porcelain-textured "boxes." "Just put your boot in the box and climb down like a ladder," Jason says, disappearing into the earth like Santa Claus. Wondering which is more terrifying, confronting your fear of heights, or losing Jason's light to the abyss, you put a tentative boot in the first calcite box and wait for it to break under your weight. When it doesn't, you put your other boot in the boxes and then your hands in the boxes until your whole body is wedged in the formation-coated crack. You can't see anything but the wall in front of you: There's barely room to turn your head. What would happen if the earth shifted? What would happen if your light went out? Jeremy sees your pause and gallantly offers to climb down in front of you and talk you through the process. You are surprised at his sixteen-year-old audacity. No, you tell him. There's nowhere to fall but down, and this crack is so narrow that if you fell, you honestly couldn't fall very far. It's really no big deal.

White Cliffs: You don't know what to call them, but they look like the White Cliffs of Dover you read about in your college humanities classes. Foot-wide slabs of limestone tower hundreds of feet in the air, encased by a stucco-like layer of hardened calcium carbonate. You can see their jagged tops, but not the ceiling beyond; nor can you see the ends of the narrow corridors they create. Sublime labyrinths: So this is your reward for being an interloper in the true caver's world! New questions keep you company: How far beneath the surface of the ocean can the White Cliffs of Dover be discerned as human-named entities? How far beneath the surface can one travel before all human significance is lost to the rocks?

Tab P340: The acid-free reflector tape is the size of a thumbnail and wedged eye-level between two rocks. You are following the survey points marked on Jason's maps. These maps are new; people have known about this particular part of the Lower Level for so short a time that none of the rooms or corridors have names yet. How many people have seen survey tab P340 in the whole history of the world? Who has seen tab P341, tab P342? Jason looks at you as if you are asking too many questions. As if you shouldn't even say "dude" when things look like the inside of a cathedral.

Rock: This is the first time you've eaten in the cave. Unless you are going on an all-day trip, food is prohibited underground because organic (i.e., associated with the living) matter left behind by humans can alter the cave's inorganic (i.e., absolutely indifferent to the living) ecosystem. Jason is eating a protein bar, and Jeremy is slurping down a strange, carbohydrate-packed gel. They talk about units of energy, units of risk precaution, the weight of amino acids. You've brought caving-smart food yourself, but you haven't gone beyond anything a normal second-grader would have in his or her lunchbox—cheese sticks, granola bars, raisins. Though you suppose it's been harder for you to fit through some of the holes with all that bulk, you are inwardly proud of your choices. You imagine your Park Service house on the surface, your ranger house-mates preparing lunch on the dishes the three of you share, eating the same food you are eating.

False Floors: "Don't step on the floors down here," Jason warns. "Some of them are only a few inches thick and are right on top of drop-offs. Chimney between the walls." You watch Jeremy pin his back to one side of the corridor, prop his feet on the other, and suspend his body in between. Moving one-half of his limbs at a time, he scoots one body length up from the false floor, then moves sideways through the corridor. Is this chimneying? You stick you elbow pads to the wall and follow suit. The white cliffs stick to the back of your shirt as if you are wearing velcro. You break a sweat fighting them but are grateful for the sense of security the friction provides. It is amazing to you how the human skeleton can calculate where each bone must be placed for optimal balance—instantly! Without any conscious thought!—when each move must be so different from the one before it. You are enjoying the miracle of your skeleton until you chimney over a place where the false floor did break. Beneath it is a gaping shaft that goes down several hundred feet. You are not allowed to be afraid.

False Floors II: More and more sections of floor seem to have fallen into the abyss. With the exposure, you are generally thirty to fifty feet from the ground instead of a single body length. You will not be afraid. Your back and elbows are getting weary of bearing the weight of your body, but they are stronger than you thought they'd be.

White Cliffs II: The boys have been silent this whole trip. Is it because they are boys? If someone would just talk you'd have something else to think about: The white cliffs you have been shimmying between are getting farther and farther apart. Jason and Jeremy don't seem to notice: their legs are longer than yours. Soon, you can no longer keep your back against the back wall but must pinion yourself between the cliffs with your elbows and the tips of your toes. You're allowed to be a teeny bit afraid now. You're glad there's food in your stomach to soak up the adrenaline. The adrenaline in your body could kill a horse.

White Cliffs III: "I feel like I'm going to fall," you say. It's the first time you've allowed yourself to admit weakness all day. You knew when you agreed to the survey trip that you weren't the physical equivalent of Jim Pisarowicz, but as a park ranger and generally healthy person, you always suspected you weren't far enough off the mark to make a big deal out of it. Apparently, you miscalculated. Jason and Jeremy look back at you, legs stretched to reach the wall, breathing consciously measured, and shake their heads. "Are your feet in a safe hold?" Jason asks, eager to keep moving. "Yes," you answer. "Are your hands in a safe hold?" "Yes." "Then you're not going to fall." You chimney a few more feet, only to feel your elbow pads slipping. You're allowed to be afraid now but you're not allowed to stop breathing. If you pass out in a corridor this deep, no one is going to retrieve your limp body. Compared to dying alone, *feeling* alone with your fear of heights is bearable. Inhale two, three, four, exhale two, three, four, inhale two, three, four. . . . Eventually you hear Jason sigh. "Jeremy, Dude, help her with footholds. I'm going to go ahead and see if I can find an alternative corridor."

Room: It has no name, but you like it. Its floor is made up of boulders instead of hollow plates—it's not false. And it's spacious as a mansion's living room—no more chimneying! You want to cry to relieve the tension of moving through that last corridor—you might as well now that you've already made a fool of yourself. But there's no time. This is the survey point Jason had in mind. "Dude, there's all sorts of leads offa here."

Hall of Mirrors: The white cliffs stand at odd angles at each end of the Room. Jason sends you and Jeremy in opposite directions with reflector tabs looking for new corridors. You feel as if you're walking through a hall of mirrors—without the mirrors—because every corner looks like the last. There are leads, but you can't walk down them for more than a few feet before they taper off or split into a passage that's already on Jason's map. You keep calling to Jason to make sure he's still in range. You hope he can hear Jeremy's voice, because you certainly can't. You imagine the boy crawling down an unknown corridor indefinitely, rendered voiceless and irrational by the prospect of virgin cave.

Little Hole: You know from research that you're supposed to be excited to crawl into a place no one has ever seen, and that you are the only one small enough to check out this lead. So you call to Jason as confidently as you can, "I'm checking out this little hole back here." "Okay, Dude," comes Jason's reply. It takes you approximately ten seconds to get your helmet caught in the tunnel, leaving you lightless and immobile. You laugh—it's heights, not claustrophobia, that's a problem for you. That's right, no worries. Boys won't have to talk you through this one. You relax all your body muscles and use flexed feet like hands to pull yourself backward and dislodge your head. Here's an image you can call up in your daydreams and return to whenever you wish: a baby delivering itself.

Upper Corridor: Jeremy has found a lead. It's up the white cliffs, just chimney up. You don't like it. Too exposed. It's narrow, so you can pinion yourself between the walls again, but now you have to keep your hands free for the measuring tape, the compass with its watery dial, the hand-held, clear plastic inclinometer: New cave does not officially exist until it is surveyed. Jason refreshes you and Jeremy on the process, which he'd introduced just before you'd gone down today. Jeremy, the lead person, will head as far forward into the unknown as he can in a straight line and attach a newly numbered survey tab to the cave wall. You will measure the distance between that tab and yourself with the measuring tape, take an angle and incline reading, and then shout your readings back to Jason. Jason will record your numbers alongside the tab number in the Wind Cave survey book. Then you will move to Jeremy's spot, Jason will move to yours, and Jeremy will move forward to a new spot to repeat the process. The three of you try. It's apparent after two readings that you don't know what you're doing. Squinting through the equipment makes you nauseated and Jason doesn't believe your numbers ("Too high Dude"). You take off your caving gloves to recalibrate the inclinometer and the next thing you know, you've dropped them into the abyss. Jeremy descends the cliffs to retrieve your protective hand gear, eager to see if there are any leads down there. Annoyed at having the process held up, Jason puts you in a different position. Now Jason shouts back Jeremy's numbers and you record, but the next thing you know, you've dropped the pencil into the abyss, and this, too, must be rescued—this time, not so eagerly. You are humiliated by the fact that your incompetence is wasting energy everyone's bodies will need for the climb back to the surface. Jason decides you should be lead person, since that doesn't involve carrying anything other than survey tabs, which fit snugly in your pocket. You go to trade places with Jeremy. He's in a parallel corridor, and the connecting corridor is so narrow that you'll have to slither through. "Come through feet first," Jeremy says.

Point of No Reference: Your head is stuck in the connecting corridor, but this is nothing like the Little Hole. Jeremy is placing your feet in footholds on the other side. He says the shaft he's pinioned in drops about sixty feet—as soon as you get unstuck, you'll have to be really careful. You don't know where your body is in relation to his. You don't know where your body is in relation to Jason's, or to Jason's map. You don't know where stories are in relation to disorientation. How will you narrate these failures of knowing to visitors? You think of the pungent smell of rain on grass, the sound of your housemates swapping stories on their way home from the visitors' center, the sight of your parents, the man you love. Wind Cave is scentless, soundless, sightless, senseless, like being dead. Where are bodies and maps and stories and connecting corridors in relation to life? This too, you do not know. You begin to cry.

Upper Corridor: You refuse to survey anymore in this—or any other— upper corridor, which means nobody gets to survey anymore in this—or any other—upper corridor because you can't survey with fewer than three people. The boys are visibly disappointed and angry, and they've been so nice to you today, and it's not their fault you can't control your fears, but they can't make you. If it's because you're a girl, so be it. You're a girl. If it's because you're a chicken, fine, you're a chicken.

Ground: At first, you want to make this downgrade up to the boys. You put good-faith effort into surveying the lower corridors. You compliment Jeremy's steady hand with the compass. You offer Jason the chocolate you stuffed in your pack at dinnertime. But eventually—about the point Jason inadvertently crinkles the cellophane of another protein bar in your ear—you stop caring about what kind of experience your companions might be having and begin owning the trip and its meaning for yourself. You call your own food breaks, climb only where you feel comfortable climbing, and take time to look at the occasional crystal formation or domed ceiling. You look at it this way: the ratio of cavers to noncavers in the world is 1 to 8,333. Most of the human population wouldn't want to have caved this long, surveyed this dangerously. These boys are lucky to have you at all.

More Ground: This is not about being a chicken or a girl: It's about being a surface dweller. Taking a secluded moment with your pee bottle behind one of the white cliffs, you turn off your headlamp and stand alone in the dark. Just like you do when you switch off the electric lights on the tour routes so visitors can get a true sense of the cave, you enjoy a shiver up your spine. You are of this Earth, the shiver says, sensate to the environment as all of Earth's creatures. But you are out of your habitat, subject to the failure of your biology down here underground. The sun will not rise to produce the energy you harvest in the plants you eat, nor will it set to signal to your brain that it is time to rest and regenerate. There will be no seasons to help you measure the passage of time and there will be no microorganisms to return your body to the Earth when you die. Go back to the surface—there, some force has created a home just for you. Suddenly, you know what it is you enjoy about that shiver: your particularity.

Hall of Mirrors: The people on the surface will be worried if you don't start heading to the elevator soon. It will take you a good three hours to get back, Jason says. So there's the Room. Then those awful, widely spaced White Cliffs. Then false floors, tab P340. Remember passing this? Remember passing that? No, you don't remember anything. Your body feels like a bruised bag of fruit, and your mind has little energy left for orientation. Your spirits, however, soar. You are on your way back to the surface, and if you make it out in the amount of time Jason predicts, you'll be able to see the last few minutes of dusk.

Boxwork Chimney: No choice but to climb back up it. No one is going to get you home but you. Your arms are amazingly strong. A hundred feet is a daunting height after ten hours of caving, but muscles bulge from your skin out of nowhere to pull you up from the Lower Level. Your legs won't give out, either. Not before you watch that sun go down on the surface. Jason and Jeremy are surprised at your speed.

Chimney Top: It's amazing to you how deep you just were—and yet how shallow in the context of the whole Earth. The sandwich-layer pictures in your ranger geology book show Earth's crust to be fifty miles thick—and that's the deli-sliciest, thinnest layer between the planet's atmosphere and its core. What small fraction of that layer did you just descend? What small fraction of the sublime do humans need to know who they really are?

Frostwork Crawl: You can already imagine this experience being over and remembering it years from now on the surface. Christmas trees: You'll remember them almost as much as your childhood holidays with your family. White cliffs: You'll remember them almost as much as your favorite books. False floors and high corridors: You'll remember them almost as much as your first ranger job, your first funeral, college graduation, and other rites of passage. Almost as much, but not quite.

Spillway: Despite your limitations, the three of you did find new cave down there, as your slimed pockets of survey tabs attest to. Jason and Jeremy can't wait to narrate its discovery to Resource Management and the local grotto. As you make your way through the Spillway—which is playful from this direction, a natural slide—the two of them talk about how excited they are to enter the survey numbers into the computer and to see the map redrawn with the corridors the three of you found. As members of that minute population that views cave exploration as the noblest of all human endeavors, they will tell the story of today's adventure like you once told Jim's and Jan's story—as an epic.

Rome: It's like stepping out of a darkroom into Disneyland. Here you are, back on the developed tour route! Jason is giddy with "how many cavers does it take" jokes. Jeremy is too new of a caver to get the jokes, which embarrasses him, which makes you laugh. You all make fun of the dirt swaths visible on your pants in the electric lights. The nearness of the elevator has gone to everyone's head.

Surface: It is still light when you get out, indigo, shadows-in-trees light, but light. It will be light for fifteen more minutes. Forgoing the ceremonial entering of data, you spend every one of these minutes outside. What will you tell the visitors about the Lower Level? You will tell them about the thousand shades of color that meet you when you return from it, the smell of the freshly rained-on grasses at dusk, the thrill of being in a world where you fully belong. Then you will send them home.

Home: Bath. Food. Stove. Sound. Dancing in your living room. Yes, you will send them home.

Siltwater

NANCY ALLYN COOK

O n THE DAY AFTER THE ATTACK on the World Trade Center I was dipping salmon along the Copper River at Chitina. I came to the Copper River because, for me, Chitina has become synonymous with salmon, because when I drive home from meetings at the Federal Building in Anchorage, Chitina is on the way. Lately my summers as a park ranger in McCarthy have become too busy for much in the way of salmon fishing. I have only a case of sockeye canned up so far—nothing in the freezer—and so I come to the Copper River in mid-September because the silvers should be running. From the dark aisles of the Chitina Trading Post, Betty, the sleepy cashier, confirms, "Sure, the silvers should be running; I don't know how hard." On September 12, 2001, I went to the Copper River for silver salmon, but I was looking for something more.

At Chitina, the Copper River rushes downstream toward Cordova with undeniable liquid violence. From the steep cliff of my dip-net perch, the river is an icy ogre writhing at a meter's distance beneath me. Glacial silts boil in the turbid water, and gusts dart up the surface like missiles as the infamous Chitina winds pummel through the mile-wide fluvial confluence. Even in my carefully chosen back-eddy, a constant tumult pulls at my ten-foot aluminum pole. One minute, the river grabs my net north toward the Wrangell volcanoes, then, next minute, something shifts, and the downstream current seizes my net and threatens to drag my own life into the icy water. So far, for me, the Copper River has been a benevolent monster only, but still, standing in proximity to its force pulls part of me back in terror.

I was sleeping at Lila's place in Anchorage when news of the suicide attacks came in across her morning radio. Lila had been at her boyfriend's the night before; she forgot to leave the key out as she had promised, and so, at 11 o'clock with a highway-driving headache, I broke into her familiar urban homestead, climbed up on the old Schwinn to squeeze through the one left-open window and straight into my familiar guest bed. In the morning, before grasping the full gravity of the news, Lila and I laughed about my antics from the night before. The attack on New York did not seem real as broadcast across her little radio. Later, I would feel my own jolt of terror when an unauthorized jet entered the restricted Anchorage airspace, and we evacuated our Park Education Specialists meeting in false alarm. Then again, that night with Lila, I watched the towers collapse on the backroom TV, and the whole event seemed more surreal than real, more like a stupid action movie than the world that we know and live in.

April, my red-haired friend at the Spirit Mountain Art gallery back in Chitina, calls me suicidal for choosing to dip-net where I do. Usually cheerful, she scolded me this morning when I told her where I was headed.

"Towards the bridge, to Howard's spot. It's the only place I have a per-mit for. Plus, Howard's nets are there, convenient and waiting."

"I hate that spot," said April, forehead scrunching as she spewed the words. "It's too dangerous. You shouldn't go there alone. But, I won't go there with you. Not to that spot."

I respect April's concerns for my safety. Like Howard himself, she is a neighbor who feels more like family than friend. But living as she does in Chitina, April's freezer is no doubt full already. My freezer is empty, and this September, dip-netting alone is my only opportunity for dip-netting at all. This September, dip-netting alone is something I know I need to do.

For many of us from McCarthy, dip-netting the Copper River is more like religion than sport, or even subsistence harvest. The long scramble up slate outcrops, over downed spruce and willow, the long scramble upriver and then the short scramble down to the cliffs at river's edge—these passages have become ritualized for me. I count on the Copper River to take me away from my day-to-day, to dwarf my human worries, and to return me to a larger self. Alone, my inner chatter is silenced by the voices of this Wrangell Mountain world. Alone, at river's edge, my senses sharpen, and with heightened awareness comes a visceral fear for my own breathing body that serves as part of the ritual's renewing process.

Parking my Subaru behind the bushes, strapping my backpack, and grabbing the old rusty spike to pull myself up the slate cliffs, I am more exhilarated than afraid. On the most exposed corner of the trail, I smile to see cliff swallow holes abundant within the sage and juniper outcrops. The last birds flew south weeks ago, but the bluffs remain alive with evidence of their summer homes. Beneath the burrows, perfectly concentric half circles are carved into the silts like hieroglyphics, and I remember when my friend Jurgen first discovered this natural pattern on a busy fishing day. At first he thought the grooves to be the work of swallows hovering outside their holes, but I argued that the wingspan was too wide, the circles too repeatedly symmetrical for a nervous bird. I hypothesized that the natural artwork was formed by one violent sweep of a predator's larger wingspan. Years ago I watched a peregrine execute the dive-bomb maneuver to earn murre chicks for an oily meal. Earlier that morning we'd watched the fighter-jet wings of falcons soaring above the Kotsina. The thought of predatory moments had me shuddering until Jurgen discovered a sagebrush root swinging back and forth in perfect pendulum.

Yes, of course, another feature shaped by the ever-present Chitina winds.

Today, on the day after the attacks on Manhattan, I marvel again at this simplest detail of wild Alaska before passing beyond the bluffs and onto the forested trail. The route to Howard's hole picks its way through prickly rose and highbush cranberry, and my fingers are bloodied by berry juice within a few minutes of walking. Halfway out I become greedy for the river, lose the proper path, and head down toward the water a hundred meters early, forcing myself to pick my way *up* through the steep brush; this trail requires greater hiking patience.

When I do reach the right spot, two dip nets stashed behind a gnarled spruce tree serve as welcoming assurance. Seeing the pile of weathered netting makes me feel part of a wild, renegade family. Above the fishing hole on the hillside is a flat spot between two spruces just large enough to pitch a tent. I have slept there while Howard dipped through the night, and I have dipped while others slept. Upstream a few meters is a big eddy tucked into the slate where my friend Elizabeth and I once tied off a raft to the butt end of a spruce log. We floated down from where the river meets the road, pulled in to fill coolers with the bright torpedo bodies of salmon, and then continued to our friends waiting at the bridge below.

This is our hallowed fishing hole, shared by a clan of friends in our McCarthy, Alaska, community. On the step stone above the main dipping hole, blood from former salmon harvests stains the slate. Tiny roe sacs cling dessicated to the stone, a reminder of summer's abundance: fresh sockeye on bonfire coals, garden salads, and rhubarb pies.

On the day after the attack on America I come to the Copper River because I crave the experience of wild natural abundance. Last night I made the mistake of listening too closely to Dan Rather and all our other media Godlords. Last night I watched too many times the fatal crashes into those famous walls of concrete, steel, and glass. "Our world will never be the same," said Rather, again and again and again.

Today I want to feel the crash of salmon slamming into my dip net. I want to witness that unchanged life force: spawn-driven fishes swimming upstream against the colossal current. Today I need to feel the fear of silt-water swirling near my lonesome boots. Today I need to be belittled by huge mountains and unending wind.

The Copper River is the most powerful thing I know here in the Wrangell Mountains. In my imagination, just like in April's, I can picture a slipped foot, an accidental fall, and the near certainty of river death. The drownings happen every year. The silt fills up your clothes; in minutes, hypothermia steals the life from your bloodstream.

In my ranger slide shows back home in Kennicott, I tell visitors from all over the world about this mighty watershed and the many glaciers that melt to feed it. The Copper is not the longest, nor most voluminous, river in Alaska, but it is the biggest workhorse of any river in our region. The Copper River is Alaska's machine of erosion and transport, the only river to breach these hundred miles of Chugach Mountains. The river corridor predates the Chugach Mountains, and because of the countless grinding glaciers of the Wrangell-St. Elias Range, the Copper carries more sediment than any river in Alaska. The glacial meltwater collected within the confines of a Mason jar reveals silt piled to the centimeter level in the bottom of a quart. In my summer slide shows I hold the settled-out liquid up to the projector's light so visitors can observe the remarkable volume of suspended sediment.

Sixty thousand cubic feet per second is a minimum flow rate of this glacial river in summer. Sometimes discharge peaks above two hundred thousand cubic feet per second, and within that constant moving body, thousands of cubic feet of silts float suspended by water in any given instant.

Two springs ago, a few miles upstream where the Cheslachina joins the Copper, I sat in the arm of a river guide named David who was just then no longer my lover. I was crying for what we could not be. He in turn was counting calmly.

"Look at the river," he said. "One-one-thousand, two-one-thousand. Sixty thousand, one-twenty-thousand, one-eighty-thousand, two-forty-thousand."

In less than twenty seconds the spring Copper conveyed a million cubic feet of siltwater; cubic miles of eroded mountain transported by river in any given year. On the day after the attack on New York, I estimate the minutes it would take for the Copper River to carry away the city blocks of dust and rubble now lying in lower Manhattan.

A month ago, in early August, I dip-netted the Copper River with my girlfriend Kris Rueter, who will be married in Manhattan this coming October. We called the fishing trip our bachelorette party; the river affirmed the abundance of love to come in her new life. In two and one-half hours "Kritter" and I pulled up twenty-eight sockeye—plus one beautiful chinook. Three times the gleeful bride-to-be dipped two salmon in one three-foot-diameter net. Three double dips, and countless times I looked downstream to see multiple green fins emerging from the gray-green surface of the river.

At the end of our bridal harvest—exhausted and elated—we fried fat pink fillets on a two-burner camp stove, minutes from dip net to skillet. I yelled a prayer of gratitude into the Wrangellia winds: "Praise the Lord and Bless the Mighty River." I come to the Copper River to feel that resilient thrill.

My friend Kris Rueter is marrying Sam Gregory, a criminal defense lawyer who works in a Brooklyn office building and who has a summer place up on the ridge above historic Kennicott. Kris and Sam met here in Alaska, but now they'll live back East for most of the year. That's been the plan anyway. A dozen of us from McCarthy bought tickets to the big wedding already. The handcrafted invitation is propped proudly on the windowsill back at my cabin. Kris is a printmaker extraordinaire; she sells her work now in that faraway Manhattan enclave that supports our nation's artists. Our McCarthy family is so proud of Kris. On the invitation her rendition of lower Manhattan's skyline sits juxtaposed against the handsome ridgeline of our local Fireweed Mountain. In her version, the twin towers stand tall as the cityscape's bi-pinnacled summit.

On the day after the attack on Manhattan, I feel horrible for Kris and Sam, for their neighbors whom I have met, and all the ones I haven't. I imagine the fear that resides thick in their bellies this morning. Thousands of human lives and a culture's very skyline have been destroyed. From my perch above the river I look upstream to the familiar mountain skyline and try to imagine how such an event would affect my still-innocent psyche. An explosive eruption of massive Mount Wrangell is my only reference point for comparison and contrast. We watch the still-active volcano blow steam each autumn. Scientists confirm that it could happen: ash-flow slurries filling the river for miles; bridges and town flushed out along its shores. How would it feel to lose our beloved landmark in an act of horrific—yet natural—destruction? How would it feel the same? How would it feel different? A volcanic eruption is horrible, but it does not intend to horrify. A volcano is powerful, but it's not power hungry.

Two summers ago I rafted the lower Copper River under the influence of the river guide David's lyrical oars. We floated away from the volcanic Wrangells and down through the Chugach Mountains. We floated down past green O'Brian Creek, down through the Woods Canyon, past Haley Creek, past Uranatina, down past Dewey Creek, past Tiekel. That raft trip was paid for by Jerry and Harriet, who own a home and business in Hoboken, New Jersey, right across the river from

Manhattan. During our days along the river, the couple spoke proudly of their vista onto the skyline, now forever infamous. Harry and Jerry, we called that pair, with huge affection. Despite Jerry's nearly paralyzing fear of bears, the couple shared a copious sense of humor.

Together we floated down past Dewey Creek, past Teikel, past Tasnuna. We floated through what they call the Big Room, down through the no-man's land of Baird Canyon and grizzly-lined Abercrombie Rapids. We floated, down, through, and out into the mountain amphitheater of Miles Lake—its miles and miles of calving glaciers.

On the last day of our July float trip, I sat with Harry and Jerry across the Copper River from the Childs Glacier near Cordova, and together we celebrated our independence as wild river pirates. Captain David drummed a salutation to the wall of calving glacier while building-sized icebergs collapsed and exploded into multistoried splashes of river water. Harry applauded involuntarily as tsunami waves of aftershock swelled across the Copper to crash into the shoreline at our feet. Jerry hooted and hollered, and all of us felt real small.

The calving activity at Childs Glacier scares many boaters into early departures from the river at the Million Dollar Bridge, but our guide, David, waited until late in the day and then braved the passage beneath the 400-foot wall of glacial ice. We waited in anticipation—holding our breaths involuntarily as we floated the mile-long stretch of river that passes beneath the frozen massif. We floated and waited until halfway down we heard the crack let loose. We waited and then we watched as a quarter-mile slab of iceberg collapsed a few hundred meters from our rafts. We watched an explosion of water I'll not forget.

In an album back home at my cabin, I have a photograph of the fear within that fearless river guide's face—his brows raised, his eyeballs bulging, his teeth exposed in a crazy grin. As he scrambled to align our boats to safety, David's fear was mixed with thrill, and then exhilaration—an aftermath of ice cubes tinkling the tubes of our still-worthy rubber vessels. In the photo, Harry and Jerry are yelping with glee while their hands remain gripped to the raft ropes in horror. Today I remember collapsing walls of glacial ice and contemplate the fine line between horror and exhilaration.

Yesterday, watching the World Trade Center towers give way and then explode again and again on Lila's television, I felt a thrill that was similar but also utterly different. The terror we felt in those rafts so near the glacier was also terrific. From my perch on the cliff, I feel the opaque river tugging at my dip net and think about Jerry in New Jersey. On our trip down the lower Copper, the factory owner could not sleep for fear of the wild mountain night. Tonight, most certainly, his insomnia returns.

On the day after the attack on America, I leave Chitina without any salmon in my backpack. My memories of rafting adventure and salmon abundance become joined with this day's request for patience and for faith. Walking the trail back to the road, I feel the pack's emptiness against the small of my back. I feel the cold air against my skin and watch one lone fish-wheel stutter in midair as wind competes with water in vehement velocity.

On the banks of the Copper River, the wind of change blows through almost every minute of every day. Soon the gray silts will settle into the gentler green stream of winter. At my safe cabin in McCarthy, a fairy ring of autumn aspens are celebrating the season of death to come. In Alaska, we live surrounded by natural forces—sometimes dangerous, but never malevolent—that keep us humble in our lives. That nature is so resilient. Those aspen leaves will survive their eight-month winter to explode green in my eyes next spring. The Copper will melt into its unsayable silty power, and the salmon will swim like missiles against the almighty water. I dip my net full for this world.

Walking North Again

GENA KARPF

I T'S A REMARKABLY DIFFICULT NIGHT where I'm camped, somewhere in the middle of a northern California wilderness. Every once
in a while I step outside of my tent and look up at the sky then look
across the surface of the small lake beside my tent. I desperately need to
see blue sky and a still lake, signaling the end to these past continuous
days of rain. Time and again my spirits crash as I see that the sky is still
a heavy gray while raindrops are falling softly onto the lake. The landscape is so bleak and barren that I wish I were anywhere else but here.
Back inside my tent, I'm hoping in vain that the clothes on my body dry
out while the sleeping bag underneath me doesn't get any wetter than it
already is. I am physically exhausted and even more exhausted emotionally. I have pain from an injury in my lower right leg, and I'm quite sure
I'll be unable to remain strong and brave even for one more day.

I'm preparing myself for another night alone. As I review the trail map
to see what lies ahead, I notice a major road I'll cross tomorrow and my
focus narrows. A brief flicker of civilization, cars passing by, day hikers
about, perhaps even a picnic area at the trailhead. This is the spark that
gives rise once again to the familiar fantasy in my mind. The I'm-
Quitting-Once-and-for-All Fantasy, which varies with each enactment,
but carries one central and unchanging theme.

It always begins in the same way. I am at a difficult point in my journey and the obstacles—both physical and emotional—feel too great to

97

bear. The pain is too much, the despair too deep, and I'm certain I can't continue. It begins with a nagging thought in the back of my mind; a demon comes to call and convinces me I cannot do this and it will be better just to give up.

In the fantasy I do go home. I strike my tent, load my backpack one last time, and walk to the nearest road. I stick my thumb out, hitch a ride to town, and get on the first flight back to my home in Anchorage, Alaska. Once I arrive at the home in my mind, I vividly see myself sitting next to a dear friend, an ardent supporter of my adventure who looks at me wistfully and says, "Gena. Why'd you do it, Gena? Why did you give up when you were almost there?"

I begin defending myself. It's vital that I be able to articulate the reason I've given up—otherwise, I feel that it means I have no honor. It would never be acceptable simply to quit and so I begin defending myself. In his entire lifetime, I wonder, does this friend possibly have enough time to sit and listen to me tell my story? Will I be permitted to tell him the reasons I should be supported for what I have achieved, rather than criticized for what I have not?

In my fantasy, I invite my friend to the trail with me so he might *feel* what I have felt day after difficult day.

Tonight at Siphon Lake completes my 120th day on the Pacific Crest Trail. I've walked 1,650 miles from Mexico, and a mere 170 miles remain until I reach my destination of Ashland, Oregon. For four months I've been walking in the wilderness, shouldering the weight of everything I have needed to survive inside a backpack that I alone have carried. Except for occasional hikers I have met along the way, I have been solo. I have woken up each day and had only the thoughts in my head to sustain my resolve to spend yet another day walking. Whether I'll walk eighteen, twenty-two, or twenty-six miles will depend upon the day, but distance has become largely irrelevant. Regardless of how far I walk, each day will still be made up of the same twenty-four hours that I will likely spend alone.

While I was planning this adventure from the comfort of my living room, I couldn't fathom how much it would hurt, both physically and mentally. I tried to fool myself into thinking I understood. Through an eight-month Alaskan winter, I'd spent hour upon hour engaged in preparation for this experience of a lifetime. My living room had become a shantytown of boxes containing everything I anticipated I'd need for four months in the wilderness. I'd been focused and fastidious in my preparations, but only time on the trail would teach me that, aside from firsthand experience, nothing could prepare me for the demands of a long-distance solo hike.

During my first few weeks on the trail, I'd begun to gain that wonderful firsthand experience. It began on May 16, 1996, as I stood at the California/Mexico border next to a monument marking the beginning of the PCT. With fear and trepidation, I took the hardest steps of my life into the chaparral landscape of southern California. Funny, I didn't remember feeling *afraid* from the comfort of my living room. I consoled myself with self-talk, "These are early days; just settle into a rhythm, your body will become strong. Take one mile at a time, just one day at a time. It's okay if it hurts. That which doesn't kill me will make me stronger."

Speaking of almost killing me, the blisters that formed on my feet are worth mentioning. I spent the first two days walking in blissful denial that I would ever get blisters, thinking that maybe I'd be one of the lucky few. On day three, that all changed when I developed blisters from heel to toe on both feet. At one point, I became so intrigued by the sorry state of my feet that I took a photo of one of them. The searing, intense pain of blisters is unpleasant at best, but it is, after all, only physical, and I learned to use my head to overcome and walk through the pain. My technique was to otherwise occupy my mind and take my focus away from my feet I thought back to my childhood growing up in a Catholic family and recalled the repetitive chanting of praying the rosary. I said a lot of rosaries through the next seventeen days.

Chafing was another notable menace during the early days of my adventure. On day one I strapped a backpack onto a body that was easily thirty pounds overweight and stepped out into the spring heat of the California desert. It took 650 miles to leave the desert behind, during which time I'd become well calloused. I lived through the chafing of my backpack on my hips, my inner thighs rubbing together, and friction in other places too intimate to mention.

I'd felt and closely watched my body change as I developed the physical strength required for a long-distance walk. I started out soft and weak, with every mile an effort, every rise in elevation a thing to fear. My legs! Ouch, my legs! Gasping for breath! Surely it had never taken this much oxygen to climb a mountain in my mind. I would lie naked in my tent at night and look past the filth and grime to examine my changing body. For weeks I saw physical pain translate into weight loss and muscular development. I became fitter, stronger. I became able to walk longer distances—ten miles, fifteen miles—before taking rest breaks. Hill climbing stopped scaring me because my breathing was no longer quite as labored. And then gradually I became aware of increasing fatigue not only while ascending but also while walking along moderate terrain. It was a different kind of fatigue than I'd known early in my walk—less muscle burning and more of a deep, draining fatigue.

However, for all of their difficulties, the physical challenges of spending four months alone in the wilderness couldn't rival the potency of the mental challenges I faced. No mental challenge was more difficult than the loneliness.

The loneliness crept in when I felt emotionally weak. I believed I should be able to rise above the physical difficulty to some serene state of acceptance. However, as much as I desired this peace with the path I'd chosen, I never did quite achieve it. When I felt strong, it was sublime; I felt as if I were the bravest, strongest woman alive. Sadly, those moments were all too few.

Undertaking a solo adventure had never been my intention, but for all of my coercion, cajoling, and persuasion, I had been unable to enlist the participation of a single other person. Nevertheless, early in my planning I'd made a conscious decision that if I were forced to choose between walking the PCT alone and not walking it at all, I would walk it alone.

Bookshop shelves the world over are filled with books extolling the virtues of silence; the Pacific Crest Trail was easily the most silent and secluded place I'd ever been. I began my walk with the dangerous expectation that over seventeen hundred miles I would live my way into the wisdom of solitude. Only in time would I come to understand that not every person is engineered for solitude. I would also come to learn that putting myself in a secluded environment alone provided no guarantee that I would embrace the silence. If people were the color in my world, how would I cope with four months in my own company?

I learned firsthand that loneliness reveals itself in different ways. I would often find myself starting a day feeling fresh, strong, and in high spirits only to begin collecting woes as the day progressed. Obstacles such as steep hills, high winds, and a blazing sun accumulated until life became the assailant and I the victim. My reserves of internal resolve were at a minimum and the smallest obstacles whittled away at that resolve until I felt I couldn't carry on any longer. I would stop walking, take off my backpack, sit on a rock, and contemplate surrendering my plan. Sometimes I would feel a deep, raw anger and scream aloud at the unfairness of it all.

Most often, though, when things got really grueling, I cried my way north. Before the PCT, I wouldn't have thought it possible to cry so much and for so many days on end. I cried because so much of the time it hurt so badly—physically hurt—and even four months into it, the walking never became easy. I cried because during so much of my walk I had no one with whom to share the beautiful moments and no one to encourage me over yet another endless string of mountain ascents. I cried because for probably the first time in my life I had to be enough for me. My resolve, my strength, my resourcefulness had to be enough and I was scared they would eventually be inadequate.

It was only later though, upon reflection, that I would come to realize that the source of most of my anger and tears was simply loneliness.

And fear. I am overwhelmed when I count the things there are to fear while spending 120 days in the wilderness, alone and largely unaided. What if I break an ankle? Am I strong enough to drag myself along miles and miles of demanding terrain to find help? What if there's a weirdo out in the woods waiting to prey on some solitary, defenseless, and unsuspecting woman? What if I encounter a bear? What if I'm struck by a rattlesnake or attacked by a California mountain lion? What if I lose the trail and get hopelessly lost? What if I can't find enough water along the hundreds of miles of southern California desert? What if I'm swept away while trying to cross a raging creek? What if I'm not strong enough to cross the PCT's eight high Sierra passes? What if the snow and ice in the mountain passes makes them impassable? What if I slip on ice and slide to my death? What if I become paralyzed by fear? Or what if, the most awful fear of all, what if I fail? What if I'm unable to walk to Oregon and consequently forced to face my friends and family and admit defeat?

So far, I've been lucky. There have been no weirdos, mountain lions, or broken ankles. I've kept my footing while crossing snow and ice. I've lost and regained the trail on numerous occasions and always found enough water to survive, even if it's meant carrying eight liters of water over thirty miles of trail. My desire to succeed has won out over fear; I've had the competency to deal with bears and rattlesnake encounters. Most important, I've not failed. Despite all adversity, I've not yet given up.

Homily for a friend complete, the fantasy ends. I feel more confident for having reminded myself of my achievements, so far having lived through every test the Pacific Crest Trail has put in my path. My courage, if it could be called that, has been my ticket to the most beautiful places I could ever have imagined—places not for the faint of heart.

My fantasy is a freedom through which I'm able to remind myself that I can choose to return home at any time; no one is holding me captive to the PCT. My journey was my choice. No one, no book, and certainly no experienced walker has ever made any pretense about this being easy. If I am honest with myself, I'll remember that I was attracted to the grandeur of the trail for the very reason that it's accessible only to those who are willing to toil and practice self-discipline.

For the moment though, I am still at Siphon Lake and my journey is not yet complete. My leg is causing me a lot of pain, rain continues into a third night, the clothes on my body are still wet, and my sleeping bag is getting wetter by the minute. To make matters worse, there is a large group of happy campers at the lake, and their jolly laughter serves only to heighten my lonesomeness. I am awake for most of the night, listening to the falling rain and repositioning my gear away from the leaks in my tent seams, weeping at the struggle of it all.

The following day, I cross the road I had seen on my map the night before. My escape. As if by design, a car is stopped on the side of the road, its occupants enjoying a picnic lunch on a rainy day. I have a brief chat with them; they are very nice and it would be so easy to ask them for a ride back to town.

Instead, I bid them farewell and walk north again. Oregon is so close.

With each desire to quit and each subsequent decision to carry on, my thoughts return to the reasons I decided to embark on this hike in the first place.

I undertook this adventure because from the time I first read about the Pacific Crest Trail at age twenty-one, eleven years before I would begin my journey, that I would walk the trail seemed preordained. I am walking because I believe in prophecy; I trust that if I'm willing to offer myself to a challenge beyond anything I've previously known, life will open new doors to me. I'm walking to develop self-confidence and give myself a reason to believe in me. At this point in my life, I desperately need a reason to believe in myself.

I'm walking for adventure, to thumb my nose at a lethargic lifestyle, and to become strong. I'm walking so that when I'm ninety years old, I won't look back with regret at not having been courageous enough to have even tried.

As on every other occasion when I've wanted to quit the trail—the first time on day eighteen and on countless occasions since—I realize that at least for the immediate moment, I've staved off my personal demons. Each time I've wanted to end my journey, I've been faced with the same choice: Will it be more painful to explain why I've quit or will it be more painful to carry on? Always, I decide it would be more painful to quit.

That it's a difficult experience isn't reason enough to quit. The pain of walking is finite. As long as I continue walking, I will reach Oregon. Living with the disappointment of failure would be infinite. To quit would be not only to fail myself but also to fail all the people who supported my aspirations. To quit would mean I was not good enough, not disciplined enough.

Over the next three days I experience the same pain in my shin, the same persistent rain, and twenty-four- to twenty-seven-mile days, all while wearing the same clothes. At long last, on day 123 the rain abates.

I am marching toward my last resupply town of Seiad Valley when I stop for a break—a gloriously dry rest stop! While resting, I pull up my pant leg and have a look at the shin that's causing me so much pain. I am surprised to find a horizontal band of swelling running around my lower leg. Peculiar, I think, for what I have self-diagnosed as an injury to a muscle that runs vertically along my shin.

I complete my walk into the tiny community of Seiad Valley. I am sixty-four miles from the Oregon border. This is where my journey ends. The following day I am diagnosed with a stress fracture to my right tibia, and I decide not to carry on the remaining three days to Oregon.

Unceremoniously and surrounded by strangers, my adventure is over.

In the end, I was on the PCT for eighteen weeks; I spent eleven of those weeks completely alone. The remaining seven weeks were spent with hikers I met along the way. No other passing hiker affected me quite as deeply as did the gentle and delightfully handsome Kris Spike from Sydney, Australia. Kris walked into my solitary camp on day forty-nine, and over the following five weeks, we would spend twelve intermittent days together. Six months later I would travel to Sydney and later propose to and marry Kris.

Prophecy reigned; life had opened the most glorious door as a reward for my conviction and discipline.

For the eleven weeks I spent in only my own company, I never did reach the state of bliss in solitude I had come to expect. I've often thought there would have been more nobility in completing my adventure without so many of the dark emotions I experienced. But then I remind myself that my adventure unfolded exactly as it was destined to. Never before had I felt so competent, so capable, and so confident in my abilities. Through every adversity, I had refused to give up.

My journey was required so I might meet face to face, in the most intimate way possible, the man who would become my husband.

My journey was required so that I might come to believe in me.

By the Sides of the Deep Rivers

KATHRYN KEFAUVER

I PLANNED TO WALK SOLO to the Gokyo Lakes to see Mount Everest. After reading *The Snow Leopard*, I would get out of bed, leave Kathmandu, and climb about 13,000 feet. I imagined the trip would take four weeks. Meanwhile I was appreciating Nepal from between the sheets. A fan whirred overhead. From my open window I could smell simmering *dhal*. Bright saris on laundry lines spanned the alley like prayer flags. Carts clacked on cobblestone. I had six weeks' vacation from my job teaching English in China, and I'd been pining for uninterrupted rest.

"A lot of expats get depressed," my American roommate in Beijing had said, noticing my after-class naps.

"I'm not depressed," I said. "I'm just tired." She was a marathon-running Californian about to begin med school, not qualified in my eyes to judge normal levels of energy.

"Twelve percent of all foreigners in China have nervous breakdowns," she said. Later she told me she'd read an article in the *Utne Reader*. "This guy in Berkeley cured his depression by getting daily foot rubs. You should read this." She handed me the magazine.

I looked at the healed man's picture: trimmed beard, Birkenstocks, sensitive eyes. I handed it back. "Someone should light a match under his foot."

Beijing had taken a toll, the biking on the gray ten-lane roads teeming with cars and cyclists, the haggling, the hassles, the back and forth to class. I'd just learned a Chinese word that meant "to drive around the road," which applied to the Beijing taxi drivers' habit of taking foreigners on long, pricey detours. It also described how I felt about myself two years out of college: driving around the road of my life.

After a year in Beijing, I missed mountain air and the absence of man-made sound. Most of all I missed fresh water. Though I'd grown up in the suburbs of Washington, D.C., I'd never forgotten the times I'd plunged into blue lakes in Montana, into my aunt's Ozark creek, into the rivers of Australia, and into the cold and rough waves off the California coast. I'd never forgotten swimming in the wild, even the times that were cold and scary. There was something about weightlessness and open space, about the constancy of water's character, even if it differed in temperature, salinity, or speed.

The sound of water, even rain on a roof, silenced the jabbering of my mind. On a raft I'd discovered pond warp, the fading of time and worry. Water bugs weren't trying to be the best. Turtles weren't swimming until they collapsed. In Beijing I'd tried unsuccessfully to sneak into a hotel pool. I even lingered in my shower, trying to get a thin lukewarm trickle to loosen the knots in my back.

So a journey to the sacred lakes of Gokyo to glimpse the world's highest peak seemed just the thing. The Gokyo Valley of Nepal, with its emerald-green water, was the less-traveled part of the Everest region. I could see myself standing at the edge of a lake, serene with the sense of arrival. I imagined the locked feeling in my limbs replaced by the lean, loose ache from so much walking. I could envision myself content, in another country. China just wasn't my place. The Himalayas, Buddhist country, was more my speed. Gautama sat under a tree for forty days; no one accused him of being depressed.

I would get out of Beijing, walk until the tired feeling wore off. Seeing Everest from the shores of the Gokyo Lakes would be my mission. I announced my plans to my roommate, and to others, spoke them too many times to change my mind.

After finishing *The Snow Leopard* and a slim volume about yeti sightings, I forced myself to wander Kathmandu's web of narrow lanes to prepare for my journey. I walked past the rows of shops selling beads, books, bowls, Buddhas, carvings, sweaters, socks, and scarves and felt myself sucked in, drawn by a force like the excess gravity of my bed.

I knew I was stalling. I half-hoped a hiking companion would materialize, despite it being the off-season. Traveling solo was part of my plan, but I hadn't ruled out meeting someone so wonderful that I'd be forced to change my mind. At the same time, I felt sick at the sight of the other Westerners in Kathmandu, getting stoned in cheap saris, devouring *lassis* and granola in front of common-room TVs, talking *dharma*. China may not have been my place, but I clung to the idea that living there made me different, that my search was unique. Besides, I'd always needed silence to hear myself think. It would be better to hike alone.

I bought two wool sweaters, then four embroidered Kashmiri shawls. I didn't need the shawls, but I couldn't stop fingering the intricate birds and branches stitched on the wool. I bought a singing bowl. I bought a red cashmere scarf, imagining myself in an American city, at night, flinging it over one shoulder. I bought new hiking boots, a new fleece jacket. The jacket I had seemed suddenly worn. It was as if I'd owned these things already but had lost them, and the kindly merchants were just giving them back.

I finally left my Kathmandu neighborhood for a day trip. I rose at dawn to walk to Boudhanath, a stone temple with a giant arched eye painted on its dome-shaped top and hundreds of prayer wheels. I walked for miles, breaking in my boots. *You came here to trek*, I reminded myself, *not to buy every fucking textile ever made.*

I passed Nepali women and girls with baskets, a buffalo hitched to a wagon. A river thinned to a creek. Cows loitered in and around the road. After four hours, I found a temple run by nuns, girls in white robes with shorn heads. The white pagoda rose from a hill overlooking green terraced valleys, the tops of trees, a horizon of jagged peaks with white snowcaps. These peaks were visible from anywhere outside the congested center of Kathmandu. The afternoon light moved in bright shapes over the tops of the mountains, glowing against deep blues and purples. For a moment the sight stunned me into sudden peace.

The little girl nuns showed me where to leave my muddy boots and led me inside a painted sanctuary. One girl held my hand. Every inch of column and roof and wall was muraled in bright red, gold, blue. A gold Buddha sat draped in flowers, cross-legged and tranquil. I imitated his pose and began to pray. *Please, help me be a better person. Let there be a point to my existence.* I felt unworthy of the place, but I didn't move. I wanted so badly to absorb the sanctuary, scorch it into my mind. I wanted to acquire it. I lost track of my prayer.

When I left I stuffed rupees into a donation box.

On the way back to my guesthouse, I stopped by the stone stairs of the Pashupatinath Temple leading down to the Bagmati River, a tributary of the Ganges. Nepali Hindus came there to pray, to bathe, to be healed, to die. At the edge of the water, a body beneath a sun-yellow drape had begun to burn. This was part of the Hindu funeral tradition, the floating funeral pyre. The belief in reincarnation meant the body in death was a meaningless shell. The family stood ankle-deep in the water, watching the raft. The flames were bright in the dusk. I felt an urge to set the whole scene in reverse, the raft floating upstream, the fire shrinking until the human shape returned, the body carried home to wake up in bed. The family would look on, eyes moist, as the first breath returned. Visitors would gather to welcome the body reborn as him- or herself. But the pyre continued to drift outward, the flames growing, the form beneath the drape visibly collapsing in the middle, caving.

The next day I stowed my belongings and set off at seven in the morning on a bus to Jiri. From there I walked and walked, steadily climbing, scurrying up and over rocks and traversing steep switchbacks. I exchanged *namastes* and smiles with women with long black hair, in blue-gray skirts and embroidered aprons, and with men carrying enormous baskets of wood on their backs. Many of them were climbing in flip-flops. I gazed over the green valleys so lush they seemed to sparkle in the morning. The brown patchwork squares of terraced fields and the human figures moving down the rows seemed to grow smaller and smaller. On narrow, upward paths I moved aside for yaks with tinny bells.

I was careful to stay hydrated, to monitor the pace of my ascent for proper altitude adjustment. I dripped iodine into my water bottle to stave off parasites. The steady motion of walking reduced sensation to the weight of my backpack on my shoulders and the burn in my calves and thighs with each upward step. For hours I looked only at my boots, which had lost all signs of newness. I stopped to absorb the view: the sloping sky over mountain peaks, the steep jagged edges, the snow in the distance. I understood how people believed the mountains to be gods.

The trails got steeper, and I stopped keeping track of the days. Rhododendron forests glowed green, and mists of clouds moved through the trees faster than I could walk. One morning a white fog thinned from the forest trail and the sunlight fell evenly in pale-yellow columns. I stopped and put my hands on the white bark of a tree, feeling its smooth aliveness as if it could feel me back. This was my reward for trekking alone. With people, I would not have stood there for as long as I did.

Through the next week, the rhododendron forests gave way to juniper scrub. My pace slowed as the air thinned. I took three-hour breaks, drinking yak butter tea, chatting with teahouse proprietors. The monsoon rains pounded the footpaths into slippery fudge. The upward scrambles required my complete focus. I didn't mind the rain; I stuck my tongue out to catch the drops. I'd purposely chosen this season to avoid crowds, and after sweating in long pants and long-sleeved shirts, I found the storms a relief. I'd packed everything in plastic bags. I liked the thunder, the bleak swelling feel of the air, the thick ropes of rain unfurling. I liked how the rain darkened the color of the stone buildings and stone prayer walls. Solitude sharpened my senses: I saw a shade of gray that actually glowed. Even though the damp made my bag heavier, sometimes I'd burst into a run.

One rainy day, I crossed a wide river on a footbridge made of old wood and worn ropes. I pulled my hands out of the dry shell of my jacket to clutch the swaying rails. I looked at the bridge for a long time before crossing, picturing myself on the rocks below, a bright pile of Gore-Tex and pale skin. Another Everest-seeker-turned-anecdote for guidebook warnings. White water rushed below, filling a pool downstream.

On the far side of the bridge, I decided to stop for the day. I entered a guesthouse, unloaded my backpack by a fire in a stone fireplace, and held my chilled fingers out to the warmth of the hearth. A Sherpa woman greeted me with the standard "*Namaste, tidi.*" "Greetings, sister." She was probably my age, late twenties, but she looked as if nothing in this life surprised her. She wore a thick wool sweater, hair in two braids, an apron. The scent of *momos*, boiled dumplings with potatoes and beans, filled the room.

Without looking at a menu I accepted her offer of *momos*, and before she left the room I learned her name was Dalma. I untied my bootlaces. When she returned I'd peeled off my socks. Five small black leeches clung to my ankles and pruny feet. My hands shaking, I burrowed through my backpack for a lighter. Dalma put down a steaming glass of yak butter tea. The metal wheel of the lighter scraped beneath my thumb. The tip sparked but wouldn't light. Meanwhile my ankles seemed to throb. I was afraid I might be offending Dalma's Buddhist sensibilities in my apparent desire to singe the leeches to death, but she pulled a pack of matches from her long apron and knelt in front of me.

"Be still," she said, gripping one ankle. With one strike, she lit a match and carefully raised it to my foot. The leech fell off, arching its body in protest. Dalma seized it between two fingernails and threw it into the fire. It sizzled. She lit another match. The flame was hot, and I yelped, curling my toes.

"Be still," she said again.

From the village of Gokyo, I made my first attempt to reach three of the Gokyo Lakes in one long climb. From the third lake I would be able to view Everest, assuming the weather stayed clear, and return to my guesthouse by the afternoon.

At the first lake, the urge to sit and sleep grew so strong I knew I would have to turn around. This was typical at oxygen-thin heights. At about 11,250 feet above sea level, my breath became short. I felt dangerously light-headed, but since I was already there, I forced myself to gaze at the emerald-green water. It was the stillest water I had ever seen, and it reflected upside-down mountains in the rock-strewn surface. Clumps of ice dotted the green, and I kept thinking I could walk over them like stepping-stones. I stood right at the edge. As I hiked back, the rumble of ice shifting echoed in the distance.

Two days later, I made it to the second lake. I hiked with a teenage Sherpa, Pemba, who was scouting on behalf of his family's trekking business. He spoke elegant English, wore jeans and hiking boots.

"Amazing," he said.

"Yeah," I said. This time, a vise-grip headache squeezed the sides of my face. I wanted to see Everest and be done with it.

"How cold do you think that water is?"

"Very, very."

"I could use a nap," I said.

"That's the altitude," Pemba said. "Keep drinking water."

The next morning I finally made it to the third lake, breathless but clear-headed. Pemba was already there. We stood in a field of boulders with residual spots of snow, the green lake, a sharp drop-off to one side, a snow-filled canyon one hundred feet below.

"There it is." He pointed to a sloping peak that angled through the clouds.

"That's Everest?"

He nodded, and I felt terror. It was just a mountaintop. It was blue-gray, almost more rounded than peaked. It didn't look different from the neighboring peaks, only slightly higher. Snow whitened the top: typical mountain. In my daypack I had only four quarts of water and clothes for a storm, but the straps seemed to cut into my shoulders. I shifted it around on my back. I needed to care about Everest. I realized how foolish I'd been, that just below the level of words, I'd thought the sight of Everest would change me. I tried to stifle the feeling of disappointment. Against my will, my face hot and my breath short, I kept thinking, *that's it?* I turned away, afraid of what Pemba might see in my face.

"That's the glacier, Ngozumpa," he said, pointing to the canyon of snow to our right. It looked like brown and white sugar. It seemed to groan occasionally, trying to move.

On the way down, I stopped again at Dalma's guesthouse. There was one other trekker—a Frenchman turned back from Everest by an expedition doctor. The climber spoke only a little English, but through pantomime and little French clucking noises, he conveyed that his irregular heartbeat disqualified him. He said his heart was broken in more ways than one. I envied him his love of Everest. We shared a dormitory room with about ten bunks, a hay floor, cedar-smelling walls.

That night I awoke so nauseated that I could barely turn over before throwing up. Finally I got outside and continued vomiting violently on a hill in the freezing night. When I tried to return to bed, I couldn't steer through the door, and without warning, I threw up on the dormitory wall.

I sat down in the mud.

The Frenchman appeared and sat outside with me until sun-up. He swabbed my sticky hair, covered my convulsive body with two sleeping bags, and tilted a glass of water to my lips. Though I never learned his name, this stranger washed my foul hair in a pot of boiled water. By mid-morning my stomach was finally calm, and I was falling asleep when he came to say goodbye. I thanked him, but I never got to say how much his kindness had meant to me.

I stayed several more days, recuperating. It was sunny and almost warm, and Dalma set a mattress and blanket on the south-facing hillside, on a steep slant above the valley. I felt how high I was, looking down on the narrow paths with yaks winding up the switchbacks I would soon descend. Though later I'd tell people I'd seen Everest, this hillside was the place I would return to in my mind. The grass was luminously green—not only were there shades of gray, but shades of green. The sun was pale yellow. I could see the trail where I had come, could see the rickety bridge and its twisting ropes. There was the river, twenty feet down the slope; I napped in the day, soothed by its ceaseless shush.

"You can bathe in the river," Dalma told me, "you just wear clothes."

She lent me a sarong, and I wore my own T-shirt.

The river was warmer than I'd expected. The afternoon was humid but I'd thought the water would be icy. The stones at the bottom were gray, brown, and mossy. Water rushed over them, leaping, holding its course. As I dunked my head, rolls of thunder outlined the steady rushing sound, and droplets of rain broke the surface. I splashed around and reclined, water to my chin, cradled in a curve of rock beneath me. As rain soaked my face, I closed my eyes. I placed my hands on the bottom, pretending I was a lizard, pretending I was a creature about to evolve. I opened my eyes and, turning over, let the current move me.

November from a Fire Tower

DOROTHY ALBERTINI

L AST FALL, MY BROTHER HAD AN EYE EXAM and was told he had a brain tumor. And so the Monday after I turned twenty-three, my twenty-five-year-old brother shuffled into pre-op at a children's hospital, surrounded by lots of much shorter patients. With the parents of these tiny people, my family and I settled into the waiting room, dumbfounded.

When my brother finally came out of surgery and we all came into his room, everyone bustled—hands everywhere—one to the towel, one to the telephone, one catching vomit, two rubbing feet, and the rest gliding purposefully around the room.

Except for me. I was in front of the door like some outsized doorstop, with my mouth agape. My mouth was wide open, and it was stuck. And there I was, looking at what had unraveled in just the last month—my brother's head, the reality of mortality—and there it was, his voice, asking someone was *I* okay. His sister, his weepy but funny and usually stable sister—he was brain tumor–tired asking was *I* okay?

In the weeks after Joe discovered his brain tumor, I sat on my bed or stood in my kitchen, wondering if I were crying or not. It's kind of like the first seconds after you've been on a trampoline—for all you know, you might still be bouncing. Or you might just be standing still. I would be talking to my mom or my best friend on the phone, and suddenly I'd have to blow my nose, and realize I had been crying the whole time because the puddle on the pillow in my lap had long since soaked through and become a stain. If I hadn't been on the phone, I wonder how long I could have cried without noticing.

When I finally had time to do something other than call a hospital or my mother or my brother's girlfriend or his friends, I decided I could climb a mountain. All of a sudden, it occurred to me that it might even be cathartic, that in all the crying, all the not-knowing, and all of the hospital trips, I had not been getting much exercise. For the first time in months, I felt happy for no reason, and I didn't even feel guilty about it. Exercise might even make me feel less numb, now that I had begun to sleep full nights and return phone calls.

So, piled in layers and colors, I drove to the base of the trail at Overlook Mountain, just outside of Woodstock, that I'd started a couple of times the summer before. This time, I would do the whole hike, and I would take my camera to the top of the fire tower and I would take pictures of the mountaintops. It seemed a fairly achievable goal, and I was excited to have thought of it.

I saw two couples coming down near the very beginning of my ascent. The first pair walked slowly, as if they'd been up since five and had unpacked a long meal from their backpacks up on the mountain. They walked as if they had no plan for the afternoon, didn't care, and wouldn't make one. The afternoon would just happen, and they'd be happy to be a part of it. The man looked straight at me, smiled. The woman's eyes drifted over from the trail to me and she nodded as they passed.

The second couple came soon after: also in their late twenties, but a little more New York City clean-cut. They both looked at me and said hello at the same time. They were moving right along. They'd overtake the organics any minute and they'd have plans for the day—probably a late-afternoon coffee with friends in Woodstock. They all looked happy. Their brothers did not have brain tumors.

Couples always make me think one of two things, the first of which is often that I wish I had someone to hike with. These couples probably woke up together. Maybe they'd be sore together the next day. The second thing is how nice it is to hike alone, and how annoying it must be to always have to pace yourself with someone else. There is no way I could have picked a start time or planned a lunch or carpooled that day. A friend actually offered to join me. And I couldn't explain why, but I didn't want him to come along. We would have ended up talking about the tumor or the weather, and I couldn't decide which seemed worse to me. I just needed to climb.

After they passed I stopped by the side of the trail to pee. It was cold—November—I did it quickly. I took off a layer as I hiked, stuffed my scarf into my backpack, drank some water. I imagined the top and the fire tower to be similair to one I'd hiked to the year before, and I guessed that the view here would be equally exciting. How could it not be? I thought, Isn't that neat, I'll climb up the tower and photograph the mountains. Look, I'm doing something. Not crying, not calling people to explain neurofibromatosis or the third ventricle or why I am so tired. I thought, Isn't it funny we have fire towers here, this is practically New England. Aren't all the fire towers in the West, where the fires are? Oh, look, I'm thinking about fire towers and dry wind, isn't that a normal thing to do; I'm still me, somewhere in here. Good, keep moving.

I reached the ruins just below the fire tower early, so I started to look around. Then I changed my mind. Finish the mountain first and then stop here on the way down and step over those Do Not Trespass signs and take some more pictures. Look at this, I have climbed a mountain, and now I will photograph it. Just around that bend up there and I bet that's where the fire tower will be. What a natural, creative thing to do.

The second I got to the clearing with the tower, the wind hit. I didn't even have time to prepare for it—I was just suddenly in the middle of it.—Climbing this mountain and then being struck by this wind at the top was like getting punched in the stomach when I was eight. Abrupt and enigmatic and it shut me up real fast.

I know nothing about hiking, but this usually doesn't stop me from doing a day hike. I like exercise, and I assume if I can get somewhere, then I can probably get back home afterward. Beyond that, I cross my fingers when I'm alone and ask lots of questions when I'm in company. I vaguely understand (when people remind me) that there are likely better times of the year to hike than others for reasons like snow in the winter and melting in the spring, but I'd never think of that on my own. So I was stupidly surprised at how icy the top of a mountain in November can be—and then there was that wind.

I have felt wind that strong once before, at my uncle's beach house on Cape Cod after a hurricane. We went outside, stood in the sand and leaned. And we didn't fall. More than anything, I felt invincible—there were all those jellyfish, washed up into rowboats on the street, and there we were, our house intact, standing barefoot on the beach, leaning at absurd angles, not falling. Like leaning into the soft end of a lion's roar. This wind though, on the top of this mountain alone in November, this was the dead center of the roaring, with no mind to stop, and the lion was twice the volume of god. Despite my paper-thin layers and my old sneakers and a trail full of ice underfoot, I still climbed the first flight of stairs on the fire tower, hoping to get a picture or two. And that wind could not have cared less about all the colors I was wearing or the winter fat I'd been saving up. Even my bones didn't feel useful on top of that mountain. Staring at my brother in his hospital bed—I had felt maybe something similar there.

He was pale, and there was a scar forming on his head that I couldn't see and a tumor beneath it, which none of us could even picture and which, for reasons not completely clear to anyone, the doctors had not removed. People who loved him held his hands, made him smile. He looked peaceful on all of his drugs, and his head must have been spinning like crazy in this tiny bed not meant for a twenty-five-year-old at a children's hospital, but he turned to my mother to ask if I were okay. Me, still mute and lead-foot at the door where I'd come in.

I remember being steered out of the room by his friends when the nurse came in to do some tests. I called my friend in Canada, told her Joe was okay. I ate lunch, stared at the floor, smiled at his friends, who left me alone, or told me stories. We went to the hospital gift shop, bought him a stuffed frog. In situations in which I am finally aware of life and death, I don't recognize myself. I look useless.

And on a mountaintop in November, I was also useless. At the top of that mountain, with my one plan that day of getting to the top and taking pictures, I barely made it to the base of the fire tower. And then stupidity got me up the flight of stairs. But when I'd stopped, it was as simple as wind—something too strong for me to stand in the middle of and not fall.

So what did I do? I ran. I mean, I bolted. My brother was somewhere in Massachusetts with a scar over the hole in his head, my mother was at home with a back sore from all the mothering, my dad was at work, and I was alone and very cold and now something very huge was practically chasing me. Down the steps of the tower, across the rock past the picnic table (was it nailed down?!), and then back to the trail, skidding and scuffling on the ice until I got low enough to walk on dirt.

A pair of men appeared, just having left the ruins, plodding along on their way to the top. These looked like normal, friendly people, people who looked as if they'd moved to Woodstock from New York City, people I'd probably like. The second man had a sunburned face, what looked like a wart on his nose; they were both in their fifties. I hoped they had better shoes on than I did. I assumed they did. They'd probably been to more hospitals than my brother or I had, probably knew how to visit someone who was wearing IVs and a gown, knew how to explain unusual tumors. Their pace was steady and slow—I bet they even stopped sometimes to look around. I smiled with all of my teeth, agreed that it was a beautiful day, and My, but it's windy up there. Of course they had good shoes on, it was November; anyone who'd been hiking before knew what it was like to be on a mountain in New York State in November. They reminded me of friends of my parents—if anything, they were probably overprepared, wore undershirts made of something I'd never heard of and socks with wicking abilities. They were fine, why wasn't I? We waved and kept walking.

And then I came to the ruins. Suddenly brave (or else embarrassed that I'd been so afraid), I stopped to have a look. I'd managed to snap only two pictures from the fire tower before I'd started to run. In the ruins, my camera got stuck and stopped winding. Too cold for my camera, too windy for me on this mountain. Too cold for my camera to rescue me from the thought of having been pretty damn close to death.

I assume it's a great thing, to be reminded like this. Good to be humiliated by unwieldy ambitions; it puts your brain back in your feet somehow. Maybe it's just lucky that I could pay attention on a mountain, and just react (and run) instead of thinking for a while. And of course it's lucky that my brother goes to work with nothing more than a scar and an MRI every three months. Certainly it's lucky that we survive as many times as we do, with or without company on the mountain.

Unanticipated Snow Cave

BARBARA J. EUSER

THE POWDER PLUMED LIGHTLY as I telemarked down the off-piste back bowls of Steamboat Springs ski area. The sky was a brilliant Colorado blue. Wispy clouds floated high overhead. A good four hours of skiing downhill through fresh powder, followed by dinner with a friend—hard physical activity outdoors plus the promise of good food and good conversation was—my idea of a perfect day!

I had slept in that morning after working late the night before. It was noon before I took the first lift to the top of the mountain. A late start—but it had taken only about four hours to do this route the one time I had done it before. Ski-bumming for the season, I skied either downhill or cross-country for a few hours almost every day. People's schedules were unpredictable. Sometimes I'd hook up with someone on the mountain, sometimes not. But I wasn't looking for company that day; it wasn't going to be a leisurely social afternoon. I wanted to ski hard for a few hours, take advantage of the beautiful day, and then get cleaned up for a date I was looking forward to.

One short, narrow section of my route concerned me. It was a drop-off right above a waterfall. Before, my friends and I had helped each other over the potentially dangerous section. Each person would station himself at the bottom of the drop-off, offer a hand, and spot the next person coming down. That way the skier coming down couldn't slip over the lip of the stream bank into the water. I began to worry about how I would get past that section skiing alone. I figured I could go very slowly, and if it looked too hard to manage on my own, I would find another route through the trees.

The deep powder that was so lovely to ski down on the steeper slopes but it stopped me as the slopes flattened out. Breaking trail slowed me. What had started out as a four-hour afternoon jaunt was turning out quite differently. Before I had even made it to the drop-off, the sun had slipped below the mountaintops. As it began to get dark, I considered my options. Far below, I could see a dirt road. I was in a drainage that looked as though it connected directly with the road. The unknown route looked simpler than the route I knew. I guessed it involved more distance, but it looked like less aggravation. Trying out an unknown route this late in the day was clearly risky but the danger of the drop-off loomed larger and larger. I convinced myself the unknown risk was less than the one I knew.

Darkness settled over the mountain. I realized I would be late for dinner and wondered whether my friend would think I had stood him up. I would just have to explain. It was taking much longer than I thought to go the "direct" way back to civilization. A side creek interrupted my descent. I would have to contour around it.

The slope was getting steep and I didn't want to lose any more elevation. I started a kick turn. I lifted my right ski up and flipped the toe to the right. I then put the ski down and transferred my weight. But as I leaned forward, putting my full weight on the ski, the ski wasn't there. I fell forward on my face and started sliding headfirst down the steep slope. My left ski was still attached to my boot and flopped back and forth as I skidded helplessly downward. My poles dangled uselessly as I tried to stop myself with my arms. My mouth filled with snow. I felt as if I were drowning.

It may have been snow accumulating in front of me that finally stopped my fall. I don't know. When I was able to breathe again, I tried to stand up but only floundered in the deep fresh powder. I had one ski and one remaining pole; I lost one pole during my fall. I didn't know whether or not my right ski had slid down the slope ahead of me. Looking down at the creek below, I realized how lucky I was to have stopped where I did. Another few seconds and I could have slid right into a "hole" in the creek—a spot the snow doesn't cover—and into the fast-flowing water.

My situation was not very good. It was dark. I had only one ski. The snow was too deep for me to make any progress at all walking—I would sink to my hips with every step. I couldn't go anywhere. On the other hand, I hadn't broken any bones. I was physically intact. I did have a day-pack with a few items in it. And I was right at the base of a tree. There was no point in floundering through the deep snow. How far would I get? With a sense of despair, I realized the best thing to do was to burrow into the snow for the night.

On the slope just above the trunk of the tree, I dug into the snow. Alternately digging and flattening the snow to create a cave that would not collapse, I fashioned a space just large enough to curl up in. I left as much of an overhang of snow as possible for insulation against the cold, clear night. I enjoy winter camping—but my previous experience had included a tent and sleeping bag. For fun, one afternoon I had built a snow cave with friends and we had sat inside with a stove and made tea. Building a snow cave for survival was something I had only read about.

Very carefully, I squeezed my five feet seven inches into the tiny snow cave. The digging, and before that the skiing, had kept me warm. But now I started to get cold. Positioned in my frozen nest, I wondered how I would get through the night. I pulled my old down jacket out of my day-pack and struggled into it. I worried about my toes. My cross-country ski boots were leather, but they were not very well insulated and a little tight. I took off my boots and stuffed my feet and boots into the daypack. The pack fabric provided a layer of insulation up to my calves. When I had set out for my afternoon ski, as a nod to emergency preparedness, I included a stub of candle, a few matches, and a couple of small Hershey bars in my pack. At the University of Colorado, I was a member of the Rocky Mountain Rescue Group. We spent hours reviewing what hikers and climbers had done wrong, thus creating emergency situations. Then we discussed what they should have done before we had to go out and search for them or pull them off the mountain. Here I wore both hats. I created the emergency by going skiing alone in the afternoon, then compounded it by deciding to try an unknown route. I was also my only rescuer, relying on what I had learned vicariously from others' errors. It was going to be a miserable night.

I stared at the walls of my tiny cave. I had on a wool hat and gloves with waterproof shells, a down jacket, and wool socks. Not too bad. But I seriously regretted wearing jeans without long underwear for my afternoon ski. I silently resolved never to make that mistake again. I thought about all the things I wished I had: a flashlight, something made of wool for my legs, a space blanket, food, a stove. My body was cooling down. I pulled my single long, brown braid around my neck, hoping for some protection.

I decided to light the candle. It might not provide much warmth, but it would at least create an illusion of warmth. I felt a flicker of pride in my strike-anywhere matches kept dry in a film canister. Too bad there were only six of them. And there weren't many places to strike them. Happily, my jeans had a metal zipper. I thought of Jack London's story. Would the roof of my mini-cave collapse if I lit the candle? I would shield the snow with my hands, collecting every bit of warmth I could. Damned if I would let the snow have any precious heat. The first match fizzled. The second match lit and I touched it to the wick. Just the sight of the tiny flame warmed me. The light changed the character of the snow cave and made it almost inviting. I nearly burned the palm of my hand as I cupped the flame. I consulted my watch. How could it be only eight o'clock?

The candle burned down quickly. I curled my fingers as close as I could to the flame, absorbing every calorie of energy. Whatever I did, I had to protect my long piano-playing fingers. When the candle was half gone, I decided I would take the chance of being able to light it again. I snuffed it out with my fingers.

Part of surviving the night would be keeping myself awake and amused as much as possible. In the light, I had rationed my two Hershey bars. I decided to eat them two squares at a time. In the dark again, I ate my first candy treat. Without candlelight, I couldn't tell how much time passed. I allowed myself another ration of chocolate, then another. Surely hours had gone by. Again, I lit the candle.

Carefully I struck the match on my zipper. Again the first match fizzled. I groaned. The second match caught. The cave was again transformed into near-cheeriness. But it was only nine-thirty. How could time pass so slowly? How could I endure an entire night of minutes that took hours to go by?

Again the candle burned quickly. I decided to burn it completely and not take a chance on lighting it successfully a third time. As before, I trapped every flicker of its warmth. Too soon, it sputtered out in the snow. I faced the rest of the night in unrelieved darkness.

Waiting as long as I could between servings, I savored each remaining square of chocolate. Finally, they too were gone. I was exhausted and colder than I had ever been in my twenty-one years. I knew I should try to stay awake. I remembered the tale of the little match girl and every other story I had heard about people falling asleep and freezing to death. I wondered how long it would take my friends to miss me. I wondered if my stood-up date would be worried, or just mad at me. Would my house-mates recognize that I was gone, or assume that I was with my friend? I wasn't supposed to be at my job cooking Mexican food at El Rancho

Restaurant again until the following evening. Via mental telepathy, I sent a personalized call for help to everyone I could think of. Finally, I couldn't keep myself awake any longer. I fell asleep shivering.

While unconscious, my soul drifted away. Instantly I understood the old spiritual, "Let Me Fly"—I was indeed flying. Flying at an extraordinarily high speed. My soul was released from my body. I could see myself lying in the little makeshift snow cave at the base of the spruce tree. I felt very sad that my parents, relatives, and friends would think I had died. They would mistake that flesh for me. Illuminated, I understood why even our miraculous bodies may be referred to as "lumps of clay." They are clay in contrast to the lightness of our souls. My soul was speeding away from its earthbound existence. I was completely happy and relieved to be released. My only regret was that people would not understand. A universe of possibilities was opening up as I raced through the darkness like a speeding star. I hadn't thought of my body as a restraint, but once freed, I recognized how confining it had been. As I sped on, I also understood that I would not turn back. The idea of spirits returning to the world made no sense. There was no way to leave a message for relatives or friends that I was happier and freer than I had ever been. Thoughts were short-circuited and came to me as flashes of understanding. There were too many levels of opportunity stretching out in front of me to waste time worrying about an earlier, inferior form of existence.

I woke up with my thigh muscles in convulsions. My whole body shook. I had been perfectly happy being released, and here I was back in my miserable body. I had been granted only a preview this time. For the rest of the night, I shivered, awake, in my cave.

As soon as the sky lightened, I unfolded myself, dug my boots out of my daypack, and struggled to put them on my feet. I was not thinking clearly, but I knew I had to start moving and climb back up the hill. Slowly, painstakingly, I worked my way up. I laid my ski across the snow, using it as a platform for my arms, while I stomped steps for my feet in the powdery fluff. As soon as I took one step up, I moved the ski and repeated the effort. My blood started circulating and I wasn't freezing anymore.

Halfway up the slope, I picked up the lost pole. Finally, I reached the spot where I had fallen. My right ski was there in the snow, ready for me to put weight on it. Forcing my fingers to fasten the bindings, I put my skis on again. Which way to go? I was afraid to continue down the drainage because other side creeks might deter me. I was also afraid to contour around the mountain and pass the narrow section I had dreaded the night before. Hungry, moving very slowly, I retraced my tracks of the day before.

I skied uphill all day. At about four in the afternoon, I crossed the rope barrier into the ski area. The lifts had closed and a snow cat was grooming the slopes. I waved my arms frantically until the driver noticed me. By radio, he informed the area office that the lost cross-country skier had been found.

That evening I learned that my friends had indeed worried and informed the sheriff's office that I had gone cross-country skiing and had not returned. When my date had shown up to take me to dinner, they realized my skis were gone. A helicopter had crisscrossed the area in the morning but had not seen me struggling in the trees. Two friends had followed my tracks, but when they saw the tracks heading down the drainage, decided I had skied out on my own. That my friends had sounded an alarm, then taken their day to ski after me, made me feel grateful and, at the same time, exceedingly embarrassed that I had put myself in such a situation.

The entire experience—from a fabulous afternoon of cross-country skiing to shivering near death in a snow cave—lasted only thirty hours. I am thankful for the fleeting preview of death, more determined than ever to savor each moment of life.

The Hidden Meaning of Fine

ANNIE GETCHELL

"**H**OW WAS YOUR TRIP?"
Fine.
There's not much more to say. I am here, apparently as whole as when I departed, though there's a cavern where my social skills used to be. Niceties, small talk, and general bullshit flushed through my larynx into the sea. Old news purged and spewed like salty spray. Dreams left untied below tide line. Indescribable sounds waver in the stratosphere thirty-five hundred frequent flier miles away. Moss creeps into footsteps. The geologic impact of my intrusion has yet to be felt.

Still, I want to be civil. There must be some image I can conjure, a scratch a snatch a patch of steely roiling sky, a sizzling silver raindrop atop copper brine . . . there must be some way to be generous with my emptiness. Slice it into portions of a size people want to nibble, taste; nothing too filling.

Just how do I explain about returning to stimulation instead of being; that my cellular level of observation is suddenly overloaded; that the macro lens I've been looking through is best not applied or it splinters into pixels rather than amoeba? How to transpose cacophonous constituents into another language? Belt sanders, referee whistles, diesel sputter, a neighbor's frustration have supplanted wind-wave-earth and creature sounds.

131

I could have you read my journal, where details cruelly skewered in a most vile and primitive way—snared with words—are mounted like trophies. If you look at them they stare back, glassy-eyed, paralyzed. You might ponder my sketches, abstract black blight upon white attempts to capture the moment when water becomes sky. Or I can just tell you the trip was fine. . . .

Which isn't really fair. So I'll try again, from the top.

This particular trip picked me one gaunt winter's day during a flight to visit my mother, then newly diagnosed with cancer. Full of thoughts about what she'd always meant to do, and the way best-laid plans get shelved, I resolved to tick off a few of my own intentions. A solo kayak journey into legendary country was high on the list.

People make journeys out of curiosity, angst, and unrelenting boredom. Some have a mission, or a message, and some go hoping they'll stumble across one. No doubt plenty step off the edge because they're afraid—and travel can suspend the inevitable reality—of seeing things as they really are, or because they are faced with an unattractive choice. Nobler excuses, say discovery or perspective or a parallel universe, are easily exposed for the sorry affliction they actually rationalize: wanderlust.

You're either a wanderer or you're not. If you are, the world is your personal enigma, and terra incognita beckons suggestively with answers to questions you never asked, only to poke holes in things you thought you knew.

But sometimes you just need a break.

So within a few months I'd procured a folding boat, booked tickets, ordered charts, packed my food, and sorted endless essentials into umpteen Ziploc bags. Above all, I avoided all temptations for brave talk. The closer the trip, the more tedious the details, the greater my ambivalence, the lower my expectations, the deeper my distractedness.

Fly cross-country. Visit a very pregnant Kristin in Portland, Oregon, and marvel how just one year before we two were traipsing about in the Wrangell backcountry, spinning romantic yarns, armed with pepper spray. Now she's heavy with new life and I'm itching to molt. Ready to get on with the trip. Pass through latte-land (Seattle) for a curbside coffee with a fellow traveling journalist *en famille*. As we exchange news and admiration, my journey presses nearer, and tears tingle my nose. I want only to sleep.

The ferry from Bellingham to Sitka provides a fascinating transition. I spend several days and nights on a four-hundred-foot boat that feels like a combination cruise ship, cargo carrier, and Noah's Ark. I marvel at slices of life: pairs of humans ideally matched, crystalline shipboard vignettes. Between sleeps there are views of shining mountains, cascades, whales, dolphin, and wide open nowhere. The famous Inside Passage is an intricate path through islands, shoals, river outlets; the piloting of the boat is quite impressive. I somehow make the acquaintance of the chief mate, who allows me into the wheelhouse during his nighttime watch. Mouselike, I study the red-lit computers, radar, and serious maritime professionals, who navigate the channels at mean low water, time arrivals like rally drivers, and dock exquisitely in midsquall. Amazingly, the ship arrives on schedule. A deckhand tosses a monkey's fist attached to a howser. My adventure is suddenly, nearly, just about, almost ready to unfold.

Two days in Sitka. I promptly find the best coffeehouse, case the hardware store, museum, waterfront; worry about the load. How will I possibly eat all this food? (I have enough for about twenty days, a few more if I stretch it.) What if the animals get to it? Will I forage, or forfeit the whole convoluted business and turn tail?

Meet a few locals, listen to their stories. Each person I talk with turns out to be Tlingit; our conversations seem loaded with odd portent, but I don't know why. I take messages from their tongues like shells and pocket them for later examination. I sense their clannish connectedness to the landscape and am vaguely envious and slightly embarrassed: Still burning for my own place I tiptoe into theirs like a timorous houseguest. One woman, a Raven weaver of baskets and ceremony, gives me a cackling, cryptic warning about the cunningness of the Land Otter People. A curmudgeonly thin-haired, thick-skinned, mostly white native hunter of sea otter reminds me with a snarl that "no one owns anything." A young salmon fisher from the Eagle clan tells me that mathematics is man's best attempt to explain relationships in nature.

I assemble my boat behind the library at five in the morning with steady commentary from a drunk white homeless boy whose two huge dogs kick sand into my kayak while they fuck. Finally, fully caffeinated and stuffed along with my gear into the boat, my trip is just one paddle stroke away. A woman from a tour boat calls over, "Are you the girl on TV?" I break for it.

Out into the channel, past the fleet, I am small, smaller, smallest. Chinook as big as my leg explode from the water all around my boat as I cross the first inlet; below me jellyfish drift like clouds in a starry winter sky. Through the first islands, around the first headland, the first reef, the second bay, the twentieth cove, I ease closer to the rocks, look for a beach, a campsite, someplace safe where I can get good and scared. I drift and listen with my guts until the water slips out from under my hull and I am tided out alongside a dead jellyfish that looks like spilled custard. Crunch up black gravel, pass an ancient shell midden, knowing there will be a campsite hidden beneath dark dripping boughs. There is.

I eat perfunctorily because I must, because the food bag weighs heavily—my dear and deadly possession. I break my silence to address the local population, whose trails showed me where to place my tent: "I see you otter and bear and squirrel. I see you have plenty and so do I; I will help you if you need it. Please leave my cache alone." Then I sleep for eighteen hours.

Wakening follows reckoning; I come alive in the midst of a crossing many days into spit and squall. Moving is effortful at first; I am offbeat of the tide. Shedding sticky webs of convenience, senses raw and exposed, I gather momentum. Everything that will be wet is wet, though there are many degrees of saturation. What will break has broken. Camera, fishing rod, I am relieved by the loss of both. For the fish fly and soar and dance about me, intent, rehearsed, yet baring everything for their grand performance. It wouldn't be sporting to arrest their dazzle on film or monofilm, to still the motion of their mission. The last thing I'd want right now is a camera looking at me.

Upon each landing I track deer, land otter, watch mink shimmy over rockweed. I apologize to raven, eagle, heron for disrupting their routine, and I gather their plumes from the surge. I sweep sticks from the moss and lay myself, a sponge upon the sponge, into the green and wonder if there is a limit to how much infinity I might absorb. And so it goes like this, ingest and purge in an orgy of expelling the old and swallowing what surrounds me. If I am defined by the space I inhabit, then the gray mist that rolls off my oily skin has rendered me a ghost. When the druids and winged messengers whisper I understand. Does this acknowledgment of mysticism make me sound self-important?

Self-serious, self-aware, self-important, self-reliant, self-centered, self-absorbed, self-confident, self-actualized, self-possessed, self-assured, selfish. Survival is all these things. If survival is living, and living is being, then it's no wonder being oneself is so bloody threatening to the collective.

And so this streaming-waking-nether-consciousness wavers between high water and low, seeps out beneath barnacle-clad basalt, streaks down the beach like tears on cheeks. But I do not weep; when skin has no edges it becomes impossible to feel forlorn.

As I slip into a creek mouth in search of fresh water, silver blue bodies crowd and bump my hull. I look down at battered thrashing sockeye stampeding against the flow. Drifting beneath them, eyeless corpses of expired soldiers scrape the gravel bed. Many are headless and eviscerated, which tells me the bears feed just upstream. Eagle sentries eye my flashing paddle from bleached snags. They are unconcerned.

I meander in my dreams and waking through silent roaring forests, past hollow trees and colonnaded roots; climb over fallen towers shrouded in brocade, part fringed emerald curtains, and pass from one labyrinth into the next. Lavender mushrooms tremble before me, ferns drape over limbs like a steward's napkin. I cannot see the eyes upon my back, but occasionally I spy a glimmer that proves I am not paranoid: cushioned in the moss, a gift. Luminous, ear-shaped whorl of abalone, wrapping of some weasel feast, now filled with duff and the tiniest seedlings.

As I work my way through my own food, I become lighter; my appetite for solid things diminishes. I sip from springs at the base of trees, tincture of bark and granite. Quench myself with tea from the needle-infused rain pooled in my tarp. The inside of me burns and I grind my teeth when I piss. If I travel far enough will I be able to exist painlessly on air like the tortoise of myth? The next step then is to lose my bones, become a jellyfish, just an aureole of salt and water and protein, kaleidoscopic systole and diastole within the sea until I enter the gentle embrace of anemone petals and the nucleus of me is consumed.

Dull metallic breath wakes me. Or maybe it is the electric charge in my thorax when an echoing *sperwhoosh* penetrates the night. Whales feed and chatter in the darkness. Come morning I set out to find them, spy on their breakfast, and for the first time long for company to share the sight of six humpbacks spouting and breeching in the current. Securely blanketed in bull kelp like a sea otter, I scan for boats. Nary a boat for days, just loaves of granite, clumsy puffins with beaks dripping capelin, and pile upon pile of driftwood.

Determined gales pin me in my cave. I wait patiently for someone to bring me French Roast with turbinado sugar and cream. Nothing happens. I pack up and move on when the wind abates, greet the Pacific swells feeling calm and unhurried. Pause to perch and pee upon unlikely ledges. Check my bearings on a gray arcing beach, a jumbled boneyard of yellow logs—animate, though somehow disembodied, stacks of amputated limbs and decapitated trunks. Move around a great headland and enter a serpentine channel eerily silent after the crashing heaving waves. Even breathing seems rude. Snake along at still slack water into the perfect circle of a protected harbor, aim for a dark break in the forest. My kayak slides in sideways with no instruction from me.

An elves' hut marks the importance of this place. Tilted and roofless, looking as though it might deliquesce at any moment. Gone is the moss chinking that once filled gaps between driftwood walls, and five-inch slugs cover all surfaces. Irreparable as an imploded beaver lodge, a place once cozy and fruitful sunk into dim legend.

Showy riled-up surf forces me into custody of the sovereign land. I walk and walk along a large animal trail, clacking a clamshell rattle to mask the pounding of my heart. Escape onto broad black slate tables compressed into layers like phyllo dough that trap tiny breast feathers of seabirds. Look out to a pedestal of broken rock to see one vast boulder split in two by a medicine man who regained his power on this very beach. A sensual tide pool shivers in the wind.

Climbing from one outcrop to another driftwood balance beam, I have no audience to see me arabesque and pivot. Picked-over deer skeletons and fish bones are strewn below. I wish for chocolate, my mother, a friend, and then decide quite firmly it is time to weave my way home. But I find I must wait for conditions.

My presence is like one wave lick, or a single claw scratch on a slimy stone. Surge enters, dribbles, belches, makes me jump. Tiny seed shells clatter and vibrant amber rockweed slurps. Puttering, no longer aware of rain, hands in pockets, I watch my wellie feet circumnavigate the island. Stalking crunching marching identifying muttering, round and down and over. I nearly miss the spectacle: A parade of fifteen land otters galumph across a slick slab and one by one *kerploop* into the sea.

A weather window opens. Despite ominous sky I creep out from around a reef, lurk in the lull of kelp, and pick my line. Recalling every lesson, I enter the surf zone, ferry up, float backward, and generally emulate the bobbing eiders that face to windward when it feels dicey. I commit the boat and ride the incoming walls of black-green rain-pocked power. Tuck into shelter and talk myself into the next set. The mercury water catches light and I am involved with the beauty. The tide and wind push me then, and I sail upon a following sea into sublime inlets and narrows. I cannot stop this homeward passage, and I rest cradled and buoyant in the swell. I pass a likely camp, unwilling to disrupt the drowsy doe curled upon the beach. Showers play hide-and-seek, hail pelts my back, a swirl of opal lifts and fluffs around petite volcanoes. Rainbows hint of trickery. Still I paddle paddle paddle on, head grows tight and pinched but there's no point—none—in stopping. To deal again with gear and decisions and brewing tea is unspeakable.

On and on, over and over the wrists flicker, sun drops, hotel room-coffee-shower-clean underwear, I pull my little boat onto the shore and stumble toward home . . .

. . . the trip was fine.

Bicycle Love

BRIANNE GOODSPEED

S OON AFTER I OUTGREW TRAINING WHEELS, I quit riding my
bike. The bulbous white helmet that my parents insisted I wear
mortified me, and since they would not let me ride outside of our
suburban Boston neighborhood, I retired both the helmet and the bike
to the cluttered basement of our house. When my mother drove, she
cursed the cyclists on the narrow New England roads. "It would ruin my
life if I killed one," she complained. When I began driving, I felt the
same way.

I went to college two hours away from my childhood home, in the
rural Pioneer Valley of western Massachusetts. The year before I graduated, I landed a job with a sixty-five-year-old biologist who let nothing
get between her and science. Dr. Margulis worked through holidays and
national emergencies, and she relied on a bike, even in snowstorms, to
get to her lab. One day I passed her as I was driving to work. She was
unmistakable, wearing a purple backpack and a long skirt. She arrived,
breathless and smiling, as I unlocked the door. This woman stood at the
threshold of her lab, holding the door open with her outstretched foot,
and began talking about termites that she had smuggled into the country from Latin America. She had the enthusiasm of a ten-year-old talking about her ant farm. She grasped my arm in excitement, compelling
me to share her delight before I started work. At that moment, as we
stood on the doorway of her lab, Dr. Margulis's vibrancy and fearlessness

transformed my life. The following weekend, I resurrected my mother's twenty-year-old blue Huffy from the basement of my parents' house.

At first, riding the Huffy felt like riding a horse. I sat upright on the wide, cushy seat as I muscled through its three working gears. Regardless of how often it was tightened, the rear brake was useless; the front brake was hardly better, and I usually had to put a foot down to stop. One day on a bike trail, when I needed to lift the heavy frame over a fallen tree, I couldn't. A cyclist waited patiently as I lifted the front wheel over the trunk, climbed over, got stuck in the branches, and then awkwardly pivoted the back of the bike over the tree.

After a year on the Huffy, I graduated from college without any provision for my future. In the same month, I ended a five-year relationship with my high school sweetheart and canceled a nine-hundred-mile backpacking trip we had been planning together. The initial rush of liberation quickly turned to panic and self-sabotage. I quit my job and gave up my apartment. I was loath to return to the world I had grown up in, but I had suddenly forsaken the one I'd created. I felt utterly uprooted.

It was Dr. Margulis, on my last day of work, who suggested I travel. The same day, I decided to take the Huffy for a three-week vacation to France.

My friend Frank, a bike mechanic, asked, "The *Huffy*? It won't be any fun. It's old. It's ugly. And it's heavy."

At the shop, he showed me a silver, ultralight Cannondale Bad Boy with super-slick tires and a beautiful frame. My heart raced. I rode around the parking lot, fumbling through a few of the twenty-seven gears, and pretended to know what I was doing. After a few minutes on the Bad Boy, the Huffy—weighty and plain—was a memory.

I was visiting my parents for a couple of days when I explained my plan to ride the Bad Boy three hundred kilometers from Paris to Centre by myself. My father discouraged me. "A new bike? You're crazy. It'll get stolen."

My mother, terrified, pleaded, "Why are you doing this? Can't you please go with one of those touring groups?"

My father added, "Did you hear about the cyclist who got run over by a bus in Boston?"

My mother nodded, "What about the woman who was stabbed to death in a restroom? She was all by herself. And she was little, just like you."

Three days before leaving, I went for a practice ride with loaded panniers and my tent on the rear rack. I obsessively planned a last-minute itinerary, and Frank gave me a crash course on how to fix a flat and repair a chain. He also showed me how to box the Bad Boy for the flight and reassemble it once in Paris, warning me to be gentle when I inflated the tires.

I panicked. I had never traveled alone; I had no idea what a derailleur was; and I couldn't speak French very well. To my fears, Frank said, "Strap a bottle of wine to your rack, relax, and remember—this trip won't make you any less attractive to men."

The woman who checked my bike at the Air France ticket counter voiced the mantra I would hear over and over, "All by yourself? You're a brave little girl."

On the plane, the middle-aged woman I sat next to looked concerned. "Aren't you afraid?" she asked.

I dismissed the question with a shrug, but I *was* afraid—of my complicated bike, of unfriendly French people, of being run over by a bus— and every time somebody asked if I were afraid, his or her fear amplified my own. I didn't see this as a vacation so much as a trial. But I didn't even know what I was trying to prove, or to whom.

The day after my arrival, I reassembled the bike in a puny Chartres hotel room, using notes I had taken during Frank's lesson. I spent the day riding through town to find the best route south out of the city. I also wanted to be in a familiar place in case the pedals or the handlebars fell off.

With the Bad Boy fully loaded, I rode through the outskirts of Chartres and got lost on streets that weren't on my map. I careened through rotaries under the strange weight of my bike, dodging tiny kamikaze cars. When an afternoon rainstorm rolled through, I stopped riding and started to cry. I walked my bike to the shelter of a nearby bus stop, where an old woman eyed me suspiciously. "What the hell am I doing?" I asked myself, as I covered my panniers with thick black trash bags and tried to find the hostel where I planned to spend the night.

I was starting to think the trip was a mistake. The bike was a limitation and I fantasized about leaving it in Chartres and hopping on a train to England. I would carry only a small backpack. There would be nothing to lock or repair. I wouldn't need to interpret French traffic laws. I missed my Huffy and the safe, eight-mile bike path I used to ride it on. Anywhere would be better than where I was. I was beginning to hate the Bad Boy.

That night, I walked through the city to the famous twelfth-century cathedral inspired by the Virgin Mary. I have never been religious, but that night I sought comfort and refuge, and I felt cast out when I discovered that Chartres Cathedral was closed. I wanted only to be inside.

Discouraged and lonely, I slumped into an empty café. I took out my map and tried to figure out where I had been and where I was going. The owner walked by my table and asked if I were lost. I thought I recognized condescension in his voice and I again fantasized about leaving France. I told him that I was cycling south and asked if he could recommend a route without much traffic. He looked at me strangely and said nothing.

After a moment, he asked, *"Tu fais du vélo? Toute seule et tu n'as pas peur?"*

"Oui," I answered. I'm riding my bike. All alone. In fact, I'm terrified.

He smiled warmly and laughed. He pointed out a route and said that in a day, I could reach Illiers-Combray, the small village where Marcel Proust once lived. He treated me to some biscuits and wished me *"Bon courage!*" when I left. I wandered through the narrow streets and returned to the cathedral for a final look before leaving town. It was still closed, but I sat down in front of it and basked in the pleasure of the café owner's kind words.

When the sun rose, strong and bright, I was already on the road after a quick breakfast of croissants and juice. By midmorning, I was far from rotaries and cobblestone streets. Rabbits darted in front of me on the long, smooth roads that cut across endless cornfields. Each town I rolled through had only a few houses, a church, a public toilet, and a bar. Old men playing *boules* stopped to stare and women looked up from their gardens as I rode by. I reached Illiers-Combray a little after lunchtime. Proust's house was, predictably, closed.

I picnicked on fresh cherries and quiche that I bought at the outdoor market. I was studying my map in the town square when an old man approached and asked me if I were lost. He recommended a route and promised that I would see only a handful of cars. He paused and asked why I was riding alone and then answered for me while I was thinking. "*Un pèlerinage,*" he said. You're on a pilgrimage.

Through the next few days, any time I took out the map—which I did often—people waited only an instant before they approached. They offered directions and phone numbers should I need any help. Several people led me to scenic routes by instructing me to follow their cars. As they zipped along the narrow streets, I pedaled hard, trying to keep up. One night, when I rolled into a small campground and set up my tent, an old couple who had been vacationing in the same spot for thirty years came over and invited me to join them for a dinner of ratatouille, bread, and wine. In the small towns I passed through—Fougerolles, Marchenoir, Morée—I met no rude waiters and saw no tourist attractions. I discovered France's alter ego: the one that loves cyclists and independence.

Four days and 120 kilometers into my trip, as a storm threatened over the fields to my right, I hit stride. The bike, which I rechristened the Bad

Girl, and I met each other head on, with no wasted energy. The speed and smoothness were intoxicating and I no longer felt as if I were pedaling. The bike and I just moved. I looked down at my legs guiding the pedals and then at my arms braced over the bars. I almost crashed, admiring how good they looked, how strong they felt, and how worthy they were of such a powerful bike.

I got a flat tire and actually enjoyed changing it. I sat on the ground with the bike next to me and spread my legs with the wheel between them, using my feet as leverage to pull the tire off the rim. I liked the feeling of yanking out the tube and scanning the inside of the tire for the offending piece of glass. When I found it, I fingered it with animosity.

That evening, when I arrived at the campground, I spent an hour before dinner tuning up the bike. I attentively tightened the brakes, oiled the chain, and rubbed the bike with a damp rag. I imagined the Bad Girl luxuriating in her attention and feeling relaxed and refreshed for the next day's ride.

Within a week, I reached the Loire Valley. I rested in Montlivault, at a secluded hostel down a dirt road. The owner, Philippe, was a thirty-six-year-old playboy with a snaggletooth that slipped over his bottom lip when he smiled. A week before I arrived, he had seduced a shy young schoolteacher named Marie, who was on vacation from Toulouse.

Since there were no other guests, Marie, Philippe, and I ate together. Philippe cooked for us and talked on and on about what a magnificent lover, skier, and citizen he was. Marie—too polite to interrupt—and I—not quick enough with the language—held our tongues, sneaked surreptitious smiles at each other, and tried not to laugh.

On Bastille Day, Philippe put on a pair of elbow-length rubber gloves, went out to the yard, and picked a bucket full of thorny weeds. Still wearing the gloves, he went into the kitchen and began preparing a special soup that, he claimed, would energize me for the ride. Periodically during dinner, he stopped talking and vigorously rubbed his chest and stomach to demonstrate how the weed stimulated his organs.

After dinner, while Marie went out to watch fireworks, Philippe and I rode our bikes to Chambord, one of the Loire Valley's many chateaux. He struggled to keep up, but the Bad Girl and I cruised ahead. The bike and I were a team. A couple. Together, we were indomitable.

As Philippe and I walked our bikes back down the dirt road to the hostel, he said that I should stay another day because love is like the Tour de France. You wait and wait and then it passes like lightning before you even know what has happened. He smiled, the rotten tooth hanging over his lip. I decided to leave that night.

I wanted to reach Pouligny St. Martin, a tiny town in Centre where I had friends. On the second day after I left Montlivault, I woke early, felt great, and decided to ride the rest of the way to Pouligny. I wrote directions on my arm so that I wouldn't need to consult the map. I stopped briefly at lunch to devour three chocolate bars and two loaves of bread and then continued to ride until late afternoon, when I noticed that the landscape was changing. It was no longer a flat easy ride. I cranked through every gear on the Bad Girl because each town I passed through had been built on top of a hill.

By six that evening, I knew that I was within fifteen kilometers of Pouligny, but I had no idea how to get there. It was so rural that it took me an hour to find another human to ask for directions. Finally, I came upon a family, repairing a lawn mower in the front yard, and asked for directions to Pouligny St. Martin.

"Pouligny St. Martin?" The father looked puzzled. They talked among themselves and then he turned back to me and said something I couldn't understand. I was silent as I fought back tears. I had been riding for ten hours. My bottom hurt, my arms were tired, and my feet were numb.

"Are you American?" the son asked in English.

"Yes! Yes! Oh my god, you speak English. Can you please help me get to Pouligny?" He spoke with his parents before he turned back to me and pointed through a mountain. "It's across the highway there. You'll see signs."

After two more hours of riding, I realized that he was wrong. There were no signs. The horses grazing on hilly pastures were picturesque, and the magnificent views from empty town squares were breathtaking, but I didn't care. I wanted to reach my friends in Pouligny. I flagged down the only car I saw and, as she gave me directions, I could tell that the woman pitied me. By the time I rolled into my friends' driveway, I was so exhausted that my body slumped over the handlebars and I could barely pedal. I stumbled inside to a warm, but bewildered, welcome, ate a pound of pasta, and fell asleep for sixteen hours.

After two days recovering, I took a train to Bordeaux, a wine region in southwest France, not far from the Atlantic coast. The train arrived on the most distant track and I had to negotiate a flight of stairs under the tracks to exit the station. I strapped my tent to the bike rack, leaned the bike against my body, and picked up the panniers in my left arm. I then picked up the bike with my right arm and walked down the stairs. I felt the rush of power that a man must feel as he grabs a girl around the waist and scoops her up onto his horse. I had a hold on the Bad Girl's frame as if she weighed nothing and were mine to control.

That evening I camped at the foot of a cliff on the banks of the Dordogne River, where I met Michel, a ten-year-old boy on vacation with his family. His eyes widened when he saw the bike. "*C'est le velo de Lance Armstrong,*" he said.

"*Non,*" I said with a laugh. It's better than Lance's bike.

Michel tried unsuccessfully to ride the Bad Girl and then stood tiptoe over the handlebars and shifted the gear levers. I watched uneasily. I didn't want to disturb his curiosity, but I also didn't want him to mess up my bike. As I struggled over what to do, I thought about my parents and sympathized with their fear about my trip. I knew that they wanted to support my experience, but that they also wanted to protect me from it. Finally, I showed Michel how the gears worked and moved the pedals with my hands so that he could continue to shift.

That afternoon, I went to the bike shop for spare tubes and a tune-up. I spent a couple of hours in spirited conversation with Bernard, an avuncular mechanic with a daughter my age, as he leisurely adjusted the gears on my bike and inflated the tires. *"Tu n'as pas peur, toute seule?"* he asked. I told him that I just had to watch out for *dragueurs*. (*Dragueurs* are French men on the prowl.) Bernard smiled and I said that at first I was scared but not anymore. As I spoke, I realized the truth of what I was saying. I wasn't afraid anymore. The terror had burned off, like calories, during the three-week ride. The bike—which at first made me feel vulnerable—now empowered me. Strangers—whom I initially found threatening—had actually gone out of their way to look out for me. Bernard gave me his phone number, directed me to his good friend, a wine merchant, and warned in broken English, "Not in the water bottle."

I spent another night by the river and stayed up late. In front of me in the moonlit water, I could barely make out a sunken German boat that the town elders insisted not be removed as a reminder of what the town had endured during the war. Around midnight, I pulled the bike inside my tent and cozied up to it. I hooked my arm over the middle of the frame, threw my leg over the seat, and was soon fast asleep.

I spent the night at the airport before I flew home, sitting next to an old woman who was traveling by herself to Russia. She saw my bike and asked about the trip. I started to cry when I told her that I didn't want to go back to the United States. She patted my knee sympathetically. *"Tu es francophile,"* she said, as if I had a terminal illness. As she dozed, I realized that she was right. I loved France for being my place of pilgrimage. I felt forever changed by it.

When I returned to western Massachusetts, there was not much awaiting my return. I spent four months looking for work and the Bad Girl began to seem like what I am not—sophisticated and sleek, efficient and high-maintenance. So, for a while, I resumed life with my darling— the old blue Huffy with a soft seat, a hopeless rear brake, and three working gears. It's the bike that I don't need to lock when I go to the library or when I leave it on the front porch at night. It is the bike that started me on the route to France.

Now, a year later, there is space in my life for dual bikes and dual loyalties, and there is also space for other things. I left both bikes at home when I accepted a job as a backwoods caretaker in northern Vermont.

One day, a middle-aged woman arrived at my drafty cabin and asked if there were a water source nearby. I could tell that she was hiking all 260 miles of the Long Trail, from Massachusetts to the Canadian border. As she stood in the doorway, something about her struck me. She had the subtle confidence of a woman at the reins of her own life. She reminded me of Dr. Margulis and, like Dr. Margulis, this backpacker was radiant with energy. I offered to walk with her to the closest reliable water source.

"What's your name?" I asked, as we negotiated the slippery trail.

"My trail name is Green Knees," she said, "because this is my first backpacking trip." She added, "But my real name is Marilyn."

"How's it been?" I asked. It was the question I asked every hiker who passed through.

"It's been everything," she replied with a laugh. Until I met Marilyn, most hikers had responded with some variation of "It's been fabulous," usually spoken with an enthusiasm that does not correspond with the reality—hunger, exhaustion, downpours—of long-distance hiking.

"So, what made you decide to hike the trail?" I asked.

She hesitated before answering. "Well," she said, "Two reasons: my marriage fell apart and I turned fifty."

I paused for a moment, appreciating her honesty, and then said, "You're on a pilgrimage."

"Exactly," she replied. "I'm on a pilgrimage."

We arrived at the spring. Water bubbled out of the mountain and over mossy rocks. We knelt and cupped our hands to drink before filling our bottles.

Later, as she hoisted her pack onto her back, I felt that her journey was also my own. It put a smile on my face to imagine Green Knees reaching the Canadian border. I wished her Godspeed and watched her walk into the woods.

First Night Out

DAWN PAUL

THERE WERE TWO WORLDS in my neighborhood. In the ranch houses and split-levels of one world, adults vacuumed rugs, dug dandelions out of the lawn, grilled hamburgers, and washed storm windows. Adults were busy and always a little tired. Their world ended where the neat backyard lawns met the scraggly oaks and underbrush of the woods.

The woods belonged to us, the kids. We ran the paths with stick rifles all afternoon. We broke the tough, woody ends of bittersweet vines and swung on them. We found box turtles in the leaves and made pens for them, in which they trudged around and around until we felt bad for them and let them go.

The woods were crisscrossed with paths and cut with shallow gullies that funneled storm water to the Pawtuxet River, an industrial stream that sometimes ran a poisonous green. There were small clearings in the woods and granite outcrops and certain trees that were good for climbing. We had named these places: Big Rock, the Crooked Tree, Suicide Hill, the Long Path. I could find my way today, decades later, from Big Rock through the mountain laurel to the river. But the last time I drove past, on some adult-world journey, there were no woods. Only new ranch houses and a road.

Adults did not enter the woods. They only stood at the edge to rake leaves into the brush or to yell for their kids to come home. Our parents

151

imagined it as a safe place, a place of sun and trees and children. And they were right. Aside from scratches, mosquito bites, cuts, ticks, bruises, poison ivy, and, once, my sister's split lip after crashing her sled on Suicide Hill, the woods were safe for children.

This explains why my parents, who were moderately watchful and protective, allowed me to spend a night alone in the woods when I was ten. It is also possible that my parents assumed I would not carry it through, that I'd run from the dark woods the way I rushed breathlessly up the cellar stairs, certain that some lurking thing was behind me. I was not a fearless child.

I was a daydreaming child. Most of my daydreams were about living alone in the wilderness, surviving by hunting, fishing, and gathering edible plants. When I was not being a pirate in the Crooked Tree or at Big Rock building forts out of scrap wood, I was preparing to live alone in the wilderness.

I brought home library books with titles such as *The Boys' Life Wilderness Guide*, *The Woods for Sam*, and *The Boy's Book of Woodscraft*. While I was chagrined by all the "boy" titles, it was clear to me that girls, with the exception of me, were not interested in living off the land alone. Their plans involved husbands and their own split-level houses. In fact, I didn't know any boys who wanted to live in the wilderness. No family in my neighborhood even went camping. As I read these books up in my reading tree, I imagined they had a very small readership of me and a handful of boys scattered across the country.

With these guidebooks, I built brush shelters and made slingshots. I dug Indian cucumber roots and chewed bullbriar tendrils. I brought home sassafras roots and boiled them for tea. My parents wondered aloud how a kid too fussy to eat eggs could eat dirty things from the woods.

When the Girl Scout troop at our church had an opening, I eagerly joined. I expected arduous hikes and lessons in making flour from pounded acorns. I had the idea that Girl Scouts were dropped into the wilderness with nothing but a jackknife and expected to make their way home. I may have confused scouting with Outward Bound.

Scouting was a disappointment. We spent most of our time in the church basement weaving sit-upons out of newspapers and making Christmas centerpieces. The closest we got to a wilderness experience was a night in big canvas tents in a field behind the troop leader's house. Six to a tent, we ate s'mores and shined flashlight shadow puppets all night. I went home with marshmallows stuck in my hair. After that, I quit scouts and continued my solitary lessons in living off the land.

One huge gap in my experience was that I had never spent a night alone in the woods. While I imagined happily trading Wonder Bread for acorn flour, I found it hard to imagine myself sleeping alone in a dark wilderness. I was often afraid at night. I slept lightly, had bad dreams, and sometimes woke in the night afraid to move or breathe. All that, despite my sister's sleeping peacefully in her bed across the room and the square comfort of the bedroom window lit by the streetlight.

If I could not sleep alone in the woods, all the rest of my imaginings— the log shelter, the meals of fresh-caught fish and fiddlehead ferns— could never happen. So one July day I mentioned casually to my parents that I would be sleeping in the woods that night. They nodded their heads in the distracted, slightly tired way of adults.

My outdoor gear consisted of a leaky one-quart aluminum canteen and a flannel-lined sleeping bag printed with repeated scenes of a tent and campfire. I rolled the sleeping bag, took a book of matches from a kitchen drawer, and found a big metal flashlight that worked by shaking it until the batteries thunked into contact. I was ready.

But it was still light outside. It was light for hours after supper. I did not want to go into the woods too early and be discovered by kids playing hide-and-seek. But I wanted to select my campsite before dark. I quietly took my gear to the steps on the side of the garage and waited. It got darker, the mosquitoes came out, and more and more kids were called home.

After shadows disappeared, but before the stars came out, I walked to the front door and put my face to the screen. My mother was sitting on the couch reading the newspaper.

"I'm going now."

"You be careful, dear. Don't go too far."

"Okay."

I stood for a minute longer. When she did not change her mind, I went back to the garage steps for my gear. I was not afraid of sleeping alone in the woods at night. I was just afraid that I might be afraid later on.

I stepped into the woods and walked down the short path to Big Rock and the Crooked Tree. I wore sneakers, no socks, shorts, and a red cardigan sweater. The sweater was hot and scratchy but the mosquitoes were fiercest at dusk. The big flashlight in my pocket banged against my thigh. I looked around at the clearing. It was trampled to dust by our playing and was scattered with scrap wood and burlap from forts built and wrecked. I could see the lights from our kitchen window through the trees.

It was not the place of my imaginings. I had pictured a secluded camp in a grassy clearing with a small cheery campfire. I had, in fact, pictured something much like the little camp scenes on the lining of my sleeping bag. My imagined wilderness camp was well away from the sight of houses, yet close enough that I could—face it—run home if I woke terrified in the night. In the daytime, this clearing had been anything I needed it to be. An imaginary jungle, the Alaskan Bush, a mountain peak. Now I needed a real wilderness.

I saw, for the first time, that my woods were not real wilderness. They were scrappy woods left behind by the house builders, full of tangled blueberry bushes and bullbriars. Standing with the canvas strap of my canteen digging into my shoulder, I noticed our broken-down tree forts and the bare dirt littered with old bike tires and rusty sled runners.

I trudged down Long Path in my scratchy sweater, lugging my sleeping bag. I walked the familiar path and looked through the thick stands of cutover oaks and maples, hoping to see an open glade I had never noticed before. I saw lights through the trees from houses, the Bennetts' and the Vincents'. In the daytime, I ran up the paths and rang their doorbells to see if Debbie or Tracey wanted to play. Looking out of the woods in the near-dark, I could no more imagine walking up to anyone's door than a raccoon or a skunk. My footsteps in the brittle leaves sounded loud. I tried to step silently, toe to heel, the Indian way of my guidebooks. A star blinked on. It seemed part of the woods, caught in the branches of an oak. It meant night had started.

The path forked and branched left down a slope. I knew the ground was muddy down there and full of stinky skunk cabbage. So I kept to Long Path, which widened out a bit. It wasn't an open clearing, but it was wide enough for my sleeping bag with a few inches on each side. I decided the path would have to make do as my camp.

I took out the flashlight and shook the batteries into place, keeping the light low so no one in the houses would see it and come to investigate. I scattered the few stones on the path and then clicked off the flashlight. Instead of comforting me, the flashlight set me apart from the woods and made me lonesome.

I unrolled my sleeping bag by touch and gradually my eyes got used to the dark. I stood the leaky canteen against the roots of an oak. I walked back down the path and squatted to pee, something I did in the daytime when I didn't want to interrupt playing to run home. I always did it quickly then, afraid a kid would come down the path and catch me. Alone in the dark, I took my time. The sissing of my pee sounded loud. I could smell it, strong, almost sweet. I felt like an animal, squatting on the path, smelling my own smells.

I took off my sneakers, set them neatly together like I did at home, and got into my sleeping bag. With my sweater rolled under my head for a pillow, I lay on my back and looked up into the dark sky. My one star was gone.

I was sleeping alone in the woods. It wasn't what I had imagined, tucked down on Long Path between the blueberry bushes with a root sticking into my back. But I was doing it.

Then, just as I'd feared, I was suddenly afraid. I stared into the dark. Lying on the ground, I couldn't even see the lit windows of houses. I was alone in total darkness. Anything could be out there. The formless creatures of my bad dreams. The lurking things from the cellar. My hands clenched. My muscles stiffened. My breath went shallow. I could not move or breathe or all of the things I imagined in the dark would reach out and find me.

I looked at the bushes and trees overhead, black against darkness, and imagined how they looked in daylight. Blueberries still hard and green. Old squirrel nests up in the oaks. I made myself picture what I knew was really out there. Mitten-shaped sassafras leaves. Old bike tires. Logs with red-backed salamanders living under them. One of my sister's plastic beach sandals. The ruffed grouse, asleep in the mountain laurel with her head tucked under a wing. And me on the ground, sucking fast nervous breaths, knees locked rigid, hands clenched to my chest.

I listened to the sound of the real woods. The breeze in the top of the oaks. The steady shrill of insects that rose and fell with my breath, which was slower now, and deeper. I cautiously reached out in the dark and found my canteen, uncapped it, and took a long metal-tasting drink. The night dew was falling. My bangs were damp. Last year's oak leaves smelled like bitter tea. I thought of the box turtles that lived in those leaves, how they pulled their hinged shells up tight. I tucked myself down in my sleeping bag and fell asleep.

The sound of rain woke me, a constant pattering on leaves. After the darkness of sleep, I could see the trees and bushes clearly, all wet and shiny. The insects had stopped singing. I knew it was very late.

The rain quickly soaked through my sleeping bag and I started shivering. I sat up. My legs and back were stiff. I gathered my gear and walked down Long Path, sure of my steps in the night. At Big Rock, I turned up the short path home. A light was still on in the kitchen window. I wondered if my parents had stayed up all night worrying about me.

I was disappointed. I had imagined waking to bird calls, the sun in my eyes. Not this wet scramble, dragging my sodden sleeping bag home before the night was over. But a little corner of me was relieved that I would not wake alone in the dark and again go rigid and breathless with fear. I was ashamed of that relief. Halfway across the soggy backyard, I turned around and faced the woods. I willed myself to walk back down the path and spend the rest of the wet night alone. But the woods were closed to me, a solid mass of darkness. I could not even see the path. The rain came down harder. I lugged my gear across the yard and went inside.

My parents were in the living room watching the eleven o'clock news. I was confused. It seemed so late. They were happy to see me. My mother said I'd had quite an adventure, and then told me to leave my wet sleeping bag in the garage for the night.

Later, in the too-bright light of the bathroom, I rubbed my face and wet hair with a sweet-smelling towel. The woods seemed far away. How long ago had I woken in the dark to the sound of rain? My big night alone in the woods, and here I was, home by eleven. I did not feel the triumph I had hoped for. But neither did I have the feeling of failure that weighed me down when I turned my back on the dark woods and trudged across the wet yard to the house. I felt only what was true. I had spent time alone in the woods at night and found real wilderness there, after all.

The Temptations of Two

SUSAN FOX ROGERS

A t SIX-THIRTY EVERY EVENING I drive the two blocks to Emily's house and together we load kayaks onto her Jeep, then drive to the Hudson River. We often put in at North Tivoli Bay, where the water, slow and cattail-choked, allows us to drift, delighted by jumping carp, a heron that takes flight, or the saucer-sized snapping turtles that rise like moving globs of algae near our paddles. Or else we take our boats to the Tivoli landing, which is not a landing at all but just a scrap of land on the far side of the train tracks with weeds and boulders and a gradual spit where we can dump our boats into the river. There, like amateur mariners, we calculate the tide—going in or out, what do you think? We could have looked this up, but neither of us worries about the tides— they are not strong enough to drag us like flotsam south to some unwanted destination. So we guess, and usually we're correct. If the tide is going out we'll head north toward the Saugerties lighthouse; if it's coming in, we direct our boats south to circle Magdalene Island.

Though these outings sound simple, even serene, at some point late in the summer, as I realized Emily was game for anything, they began to stretch. One night we created a loop by putting in at the Bays and paddling north to Tivoli, where we walked into town to get our bikes. On dirt roads, we cycled through the woods to retrieve the car. "That was a good adventure," Emily said as we loaded our boats in the dark. And she was right.

159

Ten years younger than me, Emily is slightly shorter than my five foot six, but she's much stronger because she works all day pounding nails, ripping out ugly cabinet fixtures, and making magic in people's kitchens and bathrooms. She has a tattoo on her left arm, a series of miniature quarter moons and squares that circles her smooth, firm bicep. Above this circle are some squiggles inside of a triangle, which I cannot decipher. "Don't ask," she says when I inquire. "I want to replace it with the image of a chop saw." Two weeks later she's done just that.

When we part at the end of an evening, she hugs me, an energetic, we're-kayaking-buddies hug, and I slap her back, solid like a horse's flank. Often when we're paddling we move into a spontaneous race. "You beat me because my boat is heavier," I'll complain. "I beat you because I'm stronger," she jokes, but she's right. In those moments a quirky, we're-still-kids competitiveness balloons between us. Because work outbids play, because conversations about illness—my own, those of friends, and of family—overwhelm those about health, because I am awkward in middle age, this burst of youth delights me.

And yet I resist falling into the pleasure of traveling with Emily. To me, solo is more natural than not, and at times the effort of two feels too much: two paddles, two vests, four straps. Impatience takes hold. But also with Emily I become gregarious, and talk—too much. Outdoors, where silence is one of the great pleasures, my own voice irritates me; silence is guaranteed only if I travel alone.

Emily does not go alone. When I was away during July of this summer Emily didn't paddle. "I've never been in the river by myself," she tells me. "I don't know why, it just doesn't seem safe." Her words echo as I drive alone to put my boat in at Cheviot, a small town just north of Tivoli. Emily has opted for an evening at the county fair with her sister and so that leaves me alone with a hankering to paddle and to paddle somewhere new. Though I've paddled many times alone I'm suddenly a bit hesitant. If Emily is cautious, shouldn't I be?

Earlier in the day while I was running errands a woman asked me about my red boat, perched festively atop my black Volvo station wagon. She had paddled a few times, years ago. "It's wild on the river," she said. "You have to be strong and you have to know what you are doing."

Know what you are doing.

I do know what I'm doing: I'm putting an eighteen-foot plastic boat, which seems indestructible, untippable, and unsinkable into a placid, wide body of water. Is there anything else to know? Sea monsters? Pirates? Rogue waves? My two biggest fears: ticks carrying Lyme disease, and deranged men who might attack or rape me, are not here on the water. There are sometimes a few drunks in motorboats on the weekends, but if I tuck in near shore I hardly notice them. In fact, in my boat my sense of freedom takes shape: there is wide, uncluttered space above my shoulders, and an open, gracious playground on which to move. When I think of my various solo sorties—hiking, biking, bouldering, backpacking, skiing—these in my boat seem the safest. Still, doubt creeps in: Is there something I do not know?

Late spring of this year I witnessed the ice breaking up on the river. It was a brutally cold winter for the Hudson Valley, with many days below zero, and those who know said it was the thickest ice in decades. As I stood on the bank of the river at dusk a subtle electric hum made me feel that something special was happening. The river, moving north with the tide, dragged with it large, blocky floes of ice that knocked against each other like ice cubes in a glass, only the sound was pitched higher, and on a grand scale. It was a near-miraculous sound, eerie and so utterly full of death that it shook me for days.

Until then, I had seen the river only as a playground where sailboats skimmed on windy weekends and where some came to fish. That sound and image had thumped me out of my happy complacency, had made the river infinitely more interesting. But with the warm summer days, my memory of the river's ferociousness had faded. Besides, the only thing to fear seemed to be the cold, or the crush of ice. Here in August, the water tepid, fears seemed unwarranted. Just a few days earlier I'd jumped out of my boat to see what clambering back in would entail (much clumsiness) and the water had felt like a cooled bath, though the water, silty and almost gelatinous, washed creepily over my skin. I didn't want to fall in, but if I did flip over, little harm would come of it.

At Cheviot the tide was out and the river, lapping against the concrete pull-out, looked swamp-like, stagnant. There seemed hardly enough water to float in. The parking lot, a tree-shaded strip, stood as empty as the water. With the world becalmed, my nerves provided the only snap in the air. As I undid the straps leashing the boat to the car, a man in a wide white car rolled across the train tracks, passed my car, and circled back through the lot, staring hard. "He could catch me," I thought, as I stood there, the fifty-pound boat hanging from my arms. Was this a safe place to put in? Why hadn't I asked anyone about Cheviot?

When I go alone, the questions never end. I am alert to every possible danger, human or not, and with every slip or mistake or forgotten piece of gear I remind myself of the risks. On this evening I marvel at my idiocy: why didn't I tell anyone where I was going, and when I would be home? But, by choice, I live a solitary life and there's no one to tell. Some days this creates a melancholy some would call loneliness, yet most days I think of it as freedom. Still, I could have put in at the familiar Tivoli landing, and paddled to Saugerties, a route I knew well. Why did I have to go solo and go somewhere new?

The answer is simple: I wanted to go and I wanted something new. These desires are often twinned and so too frequently I have headed out on a trail or bike ride where I did not know how hard the hills would be, if the trail would be rocky (good place to twist an ankle?), or well marked. The concerns of traveling solo were compounded by the questions of the unknown. Inevitably, I ended up bunched up with worry so that the outing was no fun. Years ago, I made a rule for myself: If you go solo, reduce the variables, go someplace familiar. It's a rule I seem to have invented only to break.

Full of a bold caution, I slide my boat into the river.

Slightly north, and across from Cheviot, stands the St. Lawrence cement plant. In the steamy late-afternoon heat, the plant's edges are blurred so that smoke and building become one billowing beige mess. There is nothing beautiful in this and I understand why everyone is fighting the construction of a new, more efficient plant in Hudson, leaving this monster dying by the edge of the water.

Despite the factory, birds near the dock thrive. A strip of rocky land juts into the river, perpendicular to the landing. On it a sycamore tips toward the water and perched there must be forty cormorants, ominous as ravens with their black wings, but goofier-looking with their long necks. Some sit with their wings spread, drying in the wind. I push into the river and turn back once to look at my car. Despite its wagon heft it looks vulnerable alone there and I think: Maybe it won't be there when I return. The comfort of the car is peculiar but real; in a child's game it would be home base, the place of safety.

I turn south, assuming that the tide must be heading back in and I'm right: Each dip into the water is deep and slow, my progress forward sure but lazy. River grass snags my paddles, so each dip is like treading, with my arms, in the thickest milkshake. To my right about one hundred yards away a green barrier separates me from the rest of the river. It's all water chestnuts, those invasive broad-leafed plants. The narrow channel I am in appears empty as far as I can see. Once I settle into my paddle I'm happy to be there. A peace descends and I notice the blue herons perched high in the trees before they swoop down, their enormous wings beating vigorously to keep their streamlined bodies in the air, their long, awkward legs extended, a narrow rudder in the wind. I pull out my binoculars and spy on the large estates, their windows open wide to this splendor.

The tranquility of the river and my steady, gentle movements have calmed my nerves, and gone is the edge that keeps me alert. My outdoor adventures are framed by that edge, half adrenaline, and half a tonic from sore muscles; when it vanishes I am at once relieved and disoriented. In that moment of calm, I usually think how to spice it up, keep the adrenaline on high. Today I consider traveling all the way to Tivoli—four or five miles—and biking back for my car. You are alone, I remind myself, don't push it. Going solo is the adventure; that is enough. Just enjoy this paddle. And I do.

After an hour, the large, white Claremont mansion with its wide, swooping lawns, appears on my left. There, seven generations of Livingstons lived and now on the five-hundred acres, people come to picnic in the summer, and cross-country ski in the winter. It is six in the evening and time to turn around. Motorboats and Jet Skis have appeared from the southwest and their high-pitched engines cut through the muted sounds of the river, which are mostly the slosh of a wake against my bow, the slap of my paddle. The engines could be irritating, but I've come to associate them—and the smell of burning oil in an outboard motor—with my time on the river. I don't like these sounds and smells, but I expect them, and in that expectation affection emerges.

I travel down the western shore, the river much deeper here where it has been dredged to allow for long freight boats, sunk low and pushed by stocky tugboats. The distance covered in an hour takes half an hour on the return. Back in Cheviot, I pull out my boat; stack it on top of the car.

Nothing happened on my outing. It was a lovely, invigorating hour and a half. The movement—my own and that of the river—has created in me a heat that is electric. It reminds me of how I felt after watching the spring break up of ice. Hot or cold, the result is the same: an excitement that tastes of fear. Here, though, the word that comes to mind is love. And why else do this? There is, of course, the love of self, one's strength and knowledge, the years of skill—a narcissistic love, a mark of the solo traveler. But this goes beyond the love of self, spills out of my thin shell; it needs an object. If someone were with me, I'd ask for a kiss. Instead, I love the river, my boat, the Catskill Mountains silhouetted on the far shore, the sound of my car as it starts so sure in the dusk.

When I step through the door of my house I walk straight to the phone: Emily, call me, I say to her answering machine, I have a new loop for us.

Emily's game. Of course. And lucky for me, her girlfriend decides to sort of but not really break up with her so not only does she want to go, she needs to go, despite the fact there is a storm warning. "I need your cynicism," she says.

As we put our boats on her Jeep, I notice her freshly cracked windshield. "This is nice," I tease. There's a long story about wood falling off the top of her car in the middle of traffic. I listen, trying not to laugh. It seems that the near-breakup has made Emily, so seemingly solid, a bit zippy. So it is not entirely out of line that when we arrive at Cheviot at six forty-five she realizes she has forgotten her paddles. I stay with the boats thinking that paddling with Emily on this evening might be more dangerous than paddling solo.

It is seven-thirty by the time we put in and by eight it's good and dark. Emily cheers when a few drops of rain fall—she wants a storm. The waves knock us around for a while and I begin to think this is all folly. Why am I following a heartbroken woman into the dark; what makes me imagine that just because there are two of us this is reasonable?

Just when I imagine saying "Let's turn back," the river settles into an almost spooky calm. We rock into our own calm as lights on shore sparkle on, and we move, quiet and strong in the water. Bugs smack into my face and I choke before swallowing a few. "Paddle backward," Emily advises and for a while we do. Free of the bugs I breathe deeply, and the texture of the air is velvet.

When we land in Tivoli, it's far past dark. "Should we drive back for your car?" I ask, and she looks at me with more disdain than I thought she was capable of. Emily has the longest eyelashes I've ever seen and a complexion that will never age so her look is, without intention, always fresh, I'd even say coquettish, if she weren't such a boy. "Okay," I say, quickly hoping she'll forget I ever suggested driving. We first collect my bike and then ride double (the first time I've done this since grade school) to her house. With my headlamp strapped on, I pedal down the empty street, lit by a fading yellowish streetlamp. Once on her bike, Emily takes off like a burst of caffeine: *Race you to the corner.* I can't resist; I fly through the stop sign chasing her.

North of town, past the large houses and the glow from living room windows, my headlamp offers the sole, frail slice of light. Emily makes me stop, turn off the light, and together we adjust to the shades of dark. "We can ride by feel," she explains. She's right: the haze from the near-full moon keeps us on the narrow county road, but the shadows from trees conceal the potholes that jar my arms in their sockets. When a car approaches, I snap on my light, tell Emily to get over, behind me.

Five miles later, I sail by the turn to Cheviot and Emily calls for me in the dark. "Where are you going?" I stop and turn around. "Good thing you were here," I say with a laugh. We pedal for a few long seconds in the dark, our fat-tired bikes rubbing hard against the cooled asphalt. "Would you have done this on your own?" she asks. "Of course," I say, exaggerating my conviction. But the words catch in my throat. "Well, maybe not the bicycling. The paddling . . . Well, probably not the paddling, not in the dark." Truth: I never would have left at seven-thirty alone, never would have paddled backward, or raced in the dark or ridden in the dark, or stood at Cheviot admiring the lights from the factory across the river. "It's fantastic, isn't it?" The monster had become beautiful, dots of light as if we'd risen too fast and our eyes had blurred.

What is safer? The folly of two or the caution of one? Neither and both. But the question is flat; safety is not why I go. There are many reasons, too obvious to mention, to venture onto the river. But always, the post-play feeling, the tantalizing heat that spreads.

Emily lay in the grass. I stretched out next to her and we watched two men fish, the tips of their poles glowing green in the night. An exquisite satisfaction took over, the kind that aches. I couldn't hug or kiss the river, the sky, the factory across the river, or my kayak, which sat five miles south, and so I kissed Emily, fast and sweet.

That abbreviated kiss seemed more dangerous than anything I'd done in a long time: The temptation of two was dismantling my edifice of one. For so long the pleasure of one was not just enough, but perfect, and now, so quick, I had been swept away by the adventurous possibility of two. I hoped that Emily might forget that what she wanted from me was cynicism: I had none to offer.

At eleven, we arrived back to load our boats. "Anyone for a swim?" I joked. How far might Emily go to drown her confusion in sweat and water and sore muscles? She waded out to her knees and stood, back to the moon and shore. "Just do it," I coaxed, not imagining she would. But before she could move, I raced toward the water and dove in.

Tough Girl

JENNIFER MATHIEU

I n THE MIDDLE OF THE NIGHT it started raining, but I was not surprised. That morning, as I had driven from Houston on the interstate heading west, the rolling purple-black clouds lined the sky like thick new carpet. All that afternoon, as I had walked alone along the Sabinal River, holding back so I would not get caught up with the other hikers, I noticed the sky getting more ominous, and I zipped up my little red hoodie and pulled down my pink wool cap. It was Texas in November, just a few weeks before my twenty-sixth birthday, and it was unnaturally cold. Rain would do little to make the situation better.

But that gray evening, after I had set up my tent and unrolled my subzero blue sleeping bag, I raced into the campground bathroom and stared at my blotchy face and rubbed the warm snot from my nose.

"I just set up a tent alone," I announced into the mirror. It could rain all night and all the next day and forever, but I had set up a tent by myself.

And so that night, at around three in the morning when the rain began to slowly drum on my temporary ceiling so loudly it woke me up, I felt giddy with success, with the fact that I was winning already.

I had planned this camping trip to Lost Maples State Natural Area in the Texas Hill Country for months, not so much because I wanted to see trees change color or spot a deer. Those would be side benefits. Mostly, I wanted to camp alone because I had decided I was not tough.

And by "not tough" I mean I was not athletic or especially coordinated, and I never had been. And by "not tough" I mean I was a *really nice*
girl, a sweet girl who everybody just loved all the time, even when
secretly I couldn't stand a quarter of my admirers. By "not tough" I
mean I was a neurotic who obsessed constantly about things that never
actually happened to her. I didn't personally know any girl who had gone
on a camping trip by herself, although I knew they were out there. And
in my mind it seemed to me that girls who tried this, who didn't need a
boy or anyone else to help them start fires, who hiked by themselves and
set up tents on their own—that those were girls who were somehow
something I was not.

Before heading out, I had told several people about my trip with the
shrug-the-shoulders coolness of somebody who had done it countless
times, as if by just announcing I was camping alone I was already under-
going a transformation. When they heard of my plans, my friends' sur-
prise and concern for me—their insistence I bring a cell phone, their
worry that I would get lost or break a leg—only made me more sure that
camping alone was exactly what I needed to do. I suppose I thought only
tough girls did scary things.

And yes, I knew it would be somewhat dangerous and risky to camp
solo, but the urge to try it, to prove to myself that I could gain some neb-
ulous quality I desperately wanted, reminded me of a strange impulse I
had once had while doing the dishes—the urge to take a large, wet knife
I had just finished scrubbing and very slowly lick the blade.

I was not completely unsuited for camping solo, at least not with regard
to the alone part. Growing up in the suburbs of Washington, D.C., I had
never been afraid of solitude, and I relished time alone by myself in my
room, where I would carefully create shoebox dioramas for no good reason, listen to the local oldies station, and practice kissing on my curled-
up hand. But I was in no way outdoorsy, and while my younger brother

and sister excelled effortlessly at every sport they tried, I dreaded gym class and had failed at organized sports at a very young age. (My mother and father signed me up for youth soccer at the age of six. I spent every game picking flowers and dancing quietly by the sidelines, while a throng of muscular children my age spared no effort to draw blood from one another.)

I did love our family trips to the beach, where we often stayed in the same rambling beach cottage each year. My room had a bedspread so orange-sherbety I would have liked to have licked it, and every day I would pull on a blue and white Speedo so worn out it was almost scandalously see-through and head to the beach. Once there, I tossed myself over and over into the waves, letting them juggle me over the gritty ocean floor.

But we didn't hike or camp or rent RVs or anything like that. My family was befuddled by other families who did such things, and I got the impression they thought it was all too much effort for something as mundane as walking in the woods.

While I was all right with being alone, in other ways I was not all right. I was a nervous little girl terrified of disappointing any authority figure—a teacher's pet with excellent grades, who, when she stumbled, could barely stand it. The year we were supposed to memorize multiplication tables and I struggled with it, I sobbed so viciously into my pillow my parents spent a few moments just staring at me before they attempted to comfort me. I worried intensely about failing in school, about failing in anything. I obsessed over terrible things happening to my family, such as the idea of my placid baby sister with the soft black curls getting kidnapped from her bed at night, or my father getting into a car accident on his way home from work. I suffered my first panic attack at age ten while watching an episode of *Punky Brewster*.

"What's wrong?" my mother had asked as I sat shaking on the couch.

"Everything," I answered.

Reading helped relax me, and so I read like crazy, sneaking books to the dining-room table and under the bedcovers. The idols of my childhood were girls who had strong bodies and could kick a ball and seemed dangerous and angry and didn't care what anybody thought of them: my favorites were Anne Shirley of Green Gables, who told off mean boys and scaled a rooftop just to prove she could, and Laura Ingalls, who slept on a prairie under an ocean of stars and played in swollen Plum Creek even when she'd been told not to. Those girls' toughness was a perfect blend of physical and emotional strength—two things I figured I was seriously lacking.

When I showed up at Lost Maples and confirmed my reservation at the welcome center, the two older women at the counter asked if I was alone.

"Yeah," I said, checking their faces for any sign of being impressed (they weren't).

After I set up my tent, I drove my beat-up purple Ford Contour to the parking area by the Maple Trail, which merged into the East Trail that led near and then over the Sabinal River. I had planned for the trip for so long that actually being there by myself in the car driving to the trailhead felt unreal to me, and I found myself smiling into the rearview mirror a lot.

I had been to Lost Maples before, but not like this. I had moved to Texas two years before to work at a newspaper, and I had fallen in love with a boy who had been camping for more than ten years. He was as laid-back as I was nervous and was a real "hard-core camper," as I liked to joke—he owned a bright yellow camp stove and a camping mattress, and he knew how to work a water purifier.

I was curious about how he could be so passionate about something I had never really tried, and when he asked me to go on a trip with him, I said yes. We started off slow, going to sites where I could take a hot shower. But soon we were camping and hiking all over the state, trekking to the top of the huge granite dome at Enchanted Rock State Natural Area and spending three nights in the Chihuahuan Desert just a few miles from the Mexican border. Serious camping exposed me to the world in a way I didn't think was possible. Sure, I had always liked nature, in the way that everyone likes bluebirds and other things that are pretty. But I would never forget the first time we drove into Big Bend National Park, in west Texas, and the sweeping Chisos Mountains and wide expanse of strange country made me literally drop my jaw.

The girl who had dreaded soccer games, and who later had hidden in the locker room during the volleyball segment of her high school gym class, was thrilled with the idea of taking trails. Hiking didn't require much more than putting one foot in front of the other, gripping my big pack, and breathing; and moving through beautiful country made my formerly awkward vehicle of a body feel agile and even strong.

But while I loved our trips, I often let my boyfriend take the lead, allowing him to pick the trails and plan the different days of our journey. And while I would have preferred hiking one mile slowly, taking in everything around me bit by bit, I kept my mouth shut even when he tried to complete a long loop trail in one day. Not that he wouldn't have welcomed my input, but the nice girl who didn't want to annoy or disappoint resisted chiming in. He was more experienced, after all.

Here, alone, I relished the idea of walking slowly, and I didn't care how far I got. As I balanced carefully on the rocks that made a path over the Sabinal, I stopped at almost every one, staring at the bigtooth maples and listening to nothing but the water moving under my feet. Eventually I found a small spring off part of the trail, and I sat there for almost an hour, periodically dipping my hand in the cold water and touching the smooth, flat stones at the bottom.

There was something a little bit dangerous about being alone on the trail, I realized, and this added a bit of deliciousness to the trip. But the danger felt vague, as if I were only experiencing it because I was a worrier, and because it had been drilled into me to feel scared as a woman alone. Could there be some madman stalking the park? Could I get lost somehow? Maybe. But to be honest, I realized I felt less afraid at Lost Maples than I had a few years before, on a crowded Chicago El train late at night, or venturing into a sweaty, drunk fraternity party during my freshman year of college.

After my hike, back at the camp, I grilled tofu hot dogs and ate trail mix. I tried to start a fire, but the wood I'd bought at the camp store was damp, and I couldn't get more than a small spark that would eventually give out. I laughed a little to myself, and when I did I realized I'd made hardly any noise all day, except for a brief conversation with a ranger and the women at the reservation desk. It was relaxing not to talk to people, not to worry about being nice or pleasant.

And it felt good and cozy to crawl into the sleeping bag and turn on the little green lantern I had borrowed from my boyfriend. I read, and I listened to the sounds of campers at nearby sites settling in. A longtime sufferer of insomnia, I fell asleep without trying at nine, and when the rain woke me up in the middle of the night, the sound of it and the feeling I got from being inside the tent I had put up all alone could only be described as perfection.

In high school, my longing for that mythical feeling of toughness only grew stronger. At home, I no longer made shoebox dioramas. Instead, my hobbies included worrying if all my girlfriends at school liked me, worrying if guys would ever like me, and writing terrible, Plathish poems in which one of the main characters always died (often in a bloody way). I said nothing to the boy who told me I gave my opinion too much in class, and I said nothing to the head of the cheer squad who suggested I was getting too fat to wear a short, pleated skirt.

I had a secret friend in high school, a girl who got bad grades and wore black—your classic high school rebellion. She was athletic and coordinated, but she'd quit the basketball team to take up with kids from the drama department. The clique-consciousness of high school prevented us from talking in class or the cafeteria, but the after-hours lessons she gave me were practically Rockwellian: She invited me to her house to read rock magazines, and she gave me my first cigarette at an elementary school playground one Friday night. I loved it—but it was like playing dress-up. I was trying on her version of toughness when it was safe and no one was looking. But I was still hiding out in the locker room during gym.

Once at college in Illinois, I embraced several of the usual suspects of post-adolescent cool—Kathleen Hanna of Bikini Kill with the word "slut" scrawled on her stomach screaming obscenities at boys from stage, Zelda Fitzgerald leaping maniacally through fountains. These girls were tough, I thought, because they were loud or complicated or depressed. I took up smoking and staring with a bored look on my face at indie rock shows. I read complicated feminist texts and bought copies of the *Worker* at the student union. I still couldn't run a mile without gasping for air, and I didn't open my mouth when I got ogled on the streets of Chicago. But I wore black fingernail polish and used the right words. I thought maybe now I was tough for real.

When I woke up the next day at Lost Maples there was frost on my car, and it was raining, hard. Most of the other campers were clearing out, ending their trips earlier than planned. Seated at my site's picnic table under the protective cover of wood, I made myself two scrambled eggs on the little camp stove, and they were the best I had ever tasted. I gulped down orange juice out of its little cardboard box and stared at the rain falling faster and faster. Because I'd forgotten to bring gloves, I periodically blew hot air onto the tips of my frigid fingers to keep them warm.

I wanted to hike again, but I decided to see if the weather would let up. And I needed to buy something to cover up my already red and raw hands. Farther down Route 187, in Vanderpool (population twenty), there was a tiny camp store where I had bought my fruitless firewood the day before. I drove down the swerving, hilly road in the rain, thinking that I should have been disappointed that the weather was so rotten, but for some reason I was not. If I wanted to leave, I would, and if I wanted to stay at my campsite in the car staring at trees through the wet windshield, I would. I could be completely selfish.

At the store there were two pairs of gloves available, hot pink or camouflage. Would a tough girl wear camo? Maybe the version of a tough girl I had admired in college would. But I chose the pink ones because I wanted to. They matched my hat.

All that morning, I drove up and down Route 187 in the rain, winding over chilly creeks and groves of bald cypress trees, driving past old cemeteries, tracking the miles between each tiny town I passed through (Utopia, population about 360; Sabinal, slightly bigger with a population around 1,700). I had stocked up on books on tape for my trip, and with my car's heat turned on full blast, I listened intently to *Shadow: Five Presidents and the Legacy of Watergate* by Bob Woodward, savoring every bit of my nerdiness.

In each small town I drove through, I stopped at the little coffee shops and ordered small meals: a grilled cheese sandwich with tomatoes, a cup of coffee, an ice cream sundae. At the café in Utopia, everyone inside was smoking except me, gossiping and complaining about the weather. I buried my face behind my magazine and fancied myself a mysterious stranger from another country. I left large tips for all the motherly women who waited on me.

Finally, around one o'clock the rain stopped, and I drove back to Lost Maples for a hike. The park was almost desolate, and I was glad for it. I wanted to climb something hard and steep, for the feeling I knew I would get in my heart and lungs, for the way it would make my nose run freely and my forehead break out in a sweat. For the view it would reward me with. So I stocked up my little backpack with a slicker, some energy bars, and a dromedary full of water, and I drove out to the trailhead.

I started in, hiking to the ponds near the point where the East Trail split in half, and I took a rest near the beginning of the steep hike to the observation point. I didn't know the elevation of the climb, only that the little paper map I'd gotten at the welcome center warned me that it was somewhat arduous. I stared out at the black pond water and realized that if I wanted to jump in and sink to the bottom, no one would ever know—not that I wanted to do that, but it was a strange thing to think about. I pictured myself from above, from the view of the God I so badly wanted to believe in, like a tiny, pink-gloved spot in the middle of that vast expanse of nature. But unlike the sense I got on crowded city streets or while trapped in twelve lanes of freeway traffic, I did not feel depressed about being swallowed up by all of it. Instead, imagining myself that way made me and my worries seem wonderfully insignificant.

After a short break, I began to hike to the top. I decided to go full force, keep a steady pace, and just climb until I made it. I had done this hike before, concentrating on the strain of my boyfriend's calves as he tromped ahead in front of me. Now there was only the ground to look at, the roots of trees, and large flat rocks that had been worn down by so many footsteps. I pushed myself, breathing loudly, and focused on the queer sensation of sweat drying almost as quickly as it appeared on my forehead. I swallowed and felt a slight, sharp pain in my eustachian tubes. I kept going. There was no way of knowing if I were getting any closer; I simply had to trust that at some point I would make the top.

"This is the story of the time I went camping alone," I thought to myself. "This will be the story of the time I hiked by myself to the top of something very big." As I moved, I thought of my eighth-grade graduation ceremony, when a girl named Joanne had read a sentimental poem she'd written about how life was a lot like climbing a mountain. And even then the words had seemed contrived and forced and silly to me, like the text on those motivational office supplies that are always for sale in airplane catalogs. But now that I was actually climbing—selecting the words I would use to tell the story later on—none of it seemed contrived in the slightest.

Finally, after about fifteen minutes, I reached the top—a small patch of rocky grass that overlooked the multicolored trees dotting Hale Hollow Creek. I pulled off my heavy wool hat and visualized steam pouring out of the top of my head, as salty drops of sweat rolled into my eyes. The bitter cold of the morning seemed as if it had happened so long ago, and I stripped off my gloves and ran my hands through my hair, slicking it back. I stood there for a good long while.

I had decided to camp alone, and so I had done it. But as I drove home the next day I was not sure that I had captured some quality I envied. Now, almost a year later, I have noticed little changes in myself. I think I'm physically tougher, in that I enjoy working out more. I go to aerobics classes at the downtown Y and sometimes I trip and stumble, but I don't mind who sees. I envision future hikes alone, or with my boyfriend, and imagine how good it will feel to be in shape for every steep climb. In the mirror I catch glimpses of muscle where there wasn't any before.

There are other changes too. Recently, I shocked myself by elbowing a drunken man at a bar who groped me and loudly telling him to leave me alone. I think of the girl I was a few years ago, and of how she would have stood there bitterly, letting him put his creepy arm around the small of her back while her cheeks burned, afraid of offending even the most offensive kind of person; of how she would have gone home and created a very poorly written diatribe on the objectification of women and cursed herself for not doing anything.

But at the same time, I think that my trip to Lost Maples made me realize that despite my tendency to ruminate over bad outcomes, despite my need to succeed, despite all of that, I wasn't really a weak girl to begin with. A weak girl doesn't fling herself into the Atlantic Ocean with giddy abandon. A weak girl doesn't traipse off to a college far from home where she knows no one. A weak girl doesn't move to a strange state to work as a journalist. And a weak girl—no matter how much tougher she thinks she still needs to become—does not plan a solo camping trip and race up a steep incline as fast as she can.

I look back on the tough idols of my past, and while some of them still ring true for me, I smile at the others I once thought to be powerful icons. Zelda Fitzgerald was a mentally ill woman married to a man who stole her ideas. What was tough about that?

Toughness can be fake—braggadocio run amok. And that sense I got by the ponds of total aloneness, of feeling microscopic—I certainly didn't feel tough in the sense that I could fight anything off; in truth I knew I couldn't. But to accept that feeling of fate, to welcome it completely, made me realize that there's even a certain kind of toughness in accepting vulnerability.

To be truly hard to break means not needing to prove that quality to anyone but me—not to my boyfriend or friends, and certainly not to the women at the camping reservation desk. To be truly tough means knowing what you want and going after it, and knowing how you feel and not rejecting it.

I think of my trip often, and I would like to camp solo again, to see what being alone in nature forces me to realize next time. I didn't take any photographs on my trip to Lost Maples, but I don't mind. Whenever I want to remember it, I need only to think of the feeling I got from standing at that point of high elevation, of staring down at the tips of trees that spread out in front of me like a crazy quilt, of being entirely in my solitude with everything I needed there, inside and around me. It was many things to me, that feeling. But mostly it was the sense of knowing that there at Lost Maples, at that moment, I was the toughest girl in the world.

Day of Listening

MARYBETH HOLLEMAN

O NLY A FEW YARDS FROM THE GLEN ALPS trailhead, the rhythmic sound of skis carries toward us. Keira lunges against the leash as a man and woman appear around the bend. Both wear large backpacks, and the man pulls a sled that bulges with gear. Though the temperature is in the teens, both are bareheaded. They are slim, red-cheeked, fit. They must be heading back in after having camped out last night somewhere up here in the Chugach Mountains, this range that rises above the flat expanse of Anchorage and the wide curve of Cook Inlet.

I'd like to do that, do some ski-in winter camping. Before moving to Alaska seventeen years ago, I couldn't imagine how to camp in snow and stay dry, because all I'd known was the wet snow of the southern Appalachians. Here on this alder-lined trail at tree line, the late March snow is so dry it squeaks with every move, a reminder that keeping dry isn't the issue—it's keeping warm. So winter camping is on my life list, my list of new things to try that I began at forty, alongside rock climbing, scuba diving, and surfing.

This ski I'm on is itself something new: to ski this route, which I haven't done since my first winter in Alaska, and to ski it alone. I often ski alone, but on groomed or well-tracked trails, and for only a few hours at a time. This is a longer trip, one that will take the better part of the day, and on a route so rarely used it's more like backcountry skiing. In summer the trail is fairly well marked; in winter it all but disappears. I may not be able to find it, but I have mapped it in my mind, and I hope my memory holds well enough.

After the campers pass, I pause to adjust my pole straps. A raven's low, guttural trill makes me look up. In a clear sky the night-black bird beats steadily toward the valley, its outstretched wings forming an arrow that points my way. To my right, a slope marked with clusters of low-growing mountain hemlock ascends to Blueberry Hill, then to Flattop Mountain, then to a line of chiseled peaks heading eastward. Before me is the broad valley that lies between them and another spiring row of peaks.

Today is Spring Equinox, that turn toward the light I look forward to all winter. It is also a Day of Listening, one of four days a year—the equinoxes and solstices—when the Alaska Quiet Rights Coalition asks people to spend some time in a natural setting recording all the sounds they hear. I like this day of listening because it forces me to pay attention; it makes me listen to more than what's going on in my own head.

Still, I'm bound to spend some time inward-listening today. It's my forty-fourth birthday, and I have a habit of asking Big Questions about my life on birthdays. To mark this turn toward fifty, I'm spending the day alone, doing something new, something that pushes up against the edge of my comfort zone.

I'm not an athlete. I haven't been on a team since water polo in ninth grade, and I don't have a regular exercise routine. I ski, kayak, bike, swim, hike—but all sporadically, and none particularly well. Weekend warrior? Not even that. Entire weekends go by with my barely getting out to walk the dog.

As I've turned older, though, I've become more interested in being strong than in looking good. Not that I ever spent much time trying to look attractive—I never caught on to the routines of wearing makeup or fixing my hair or even keeping up with fashion. The idea of being strong, however, has been gaining momentum. On a run last summer, I was suddenly aware of my beating heart. How many times in my life had it already beat? How many more times might it? This blood coursing through my body, this one muscle pumping all of it, all the time, keeping me alive: each beat of my heart is in direct response to the choices I make every day of my life.

My body changes with the years. The skin grows less elastic, the eyelids and cheeks and belly and breasts all feel the pull of gravity. White hairs sprout along my temples, new hairs appear along the naval line, around the nipples. They are wiry, stronger than my more familiar browns. I like them. I want to be as strong and tough as my new white hairs.

On this birthday, this equinox, this day for listening, all I've brought with me is my dog, a strong and stubborn Siberian husky who will stay with me only if she's leashed. This necessitates our version of skijoring: Keira is attached to me by a retractable leash hooked into my belly pack. Most of the time, this keeps her in front of me. But if there's a vole or squirrel off-trail, she'll suddenly pounce and tear off into the woods while I come to a screeching stop with as much grace as I can summon in a split second. She pulls only downhill; uphill, she slows to a trot, keeping the line slack. Not only does she make downhills faster, but also less controllable, for as long as I'm careening behind her, she won't, no matter what expletives I yell, slow down. I think she's afraid I might run into her; she's a pretty smart husky.

Still, with three inches of fresh snow, the trail should be slower, and since it's been below freezing for weeks, there's little chance of icy patches on all but the most heavily trod trails. This first section is wide and well worn, one of the closest above–tree line trailheads within a short drive of Anchorage. Already at nine in the morning, it's etched with several new tracks. I let my skis fall into them, excited to have pulled off this adventure, to have this entire sun-drenched day all to myself. The trail and weather are nearly perfect, and I move with a rhythm that matches Keira's quick pace.

Within an hour, I cut off the wide trail that continues up-valley to the pass and then down into Indian. I'll ski down to and across the creek that courses through the valley, and turn northwest to traverse the flanks of several mountains in the Chugach's front range. My route will roughly follow Campbell Creek as it is joined by several other forks and descends from tundra into spruce forest. I'll finish just before the creek plunges into a gorge, meanders through the Anchorage Bowl, and pours into Cook Inlet.

This side trail hasn't been tracked at all, and I quickly lose any sign of it. Keira bounds downhill, her thick black and white tail like a flag before me, following the most direct but steepest route. I manage to rein her in and stop on the crest of a hill, trying to discern the best way down. The last thing I want to do is shoot down so fast that we fly into the creek. It's not frozen solid; even at this distance there's a faint gurgling of water pushing under ice.

There is no good way. We've overshot the trail so far that all that's left to do is aim for the bridge and head straight down. I determine to try a bit of semi-telemarking—curving from side to side, slowing the descent a bit. Keira has no such plans. We tear downhill and then—*whump*—I fall and sink into a drift, all but my head covered in snow.

I'm pissed at Keira, my throat aching from yelling at her to slow down. But what did I expect? This is what she does, and I've never, even after training classes and years of trying, been able to coerce her into obedience. I could have left her at home, could have skied down this hill under my own power—and control—without a spill.

But I could no more leave Keira behind than I could leave behind my right ski. Keira lives for these outings; more than any dog I've known, she absolutely needs to run. I once met another Siberian husky owner who said he ran five miles a day with his dog. It was still, he said, not enough. Knowing how much these dogs need to run, knowing I don't come anywhere near five miles a day, I take her with me everywhere. She even rides in my car, preferring to sit in it all day, on the chance we'll stop for a walk on the way home, than to stay alone in our one-acre fenced yard. Keira is with me so much that when I go solo, I go with her.

I chose this wild blue-eyed dog just as I chose to be a writer, a wife, an Alaskan, a mother. Grain and chaff together. Having so chosen, here I am, tumbled into a snowdrift. This is not the first time my allegiance to Keira has led me beyond the boundaries of sane behavior.

I'm also angry at myself, for falling, for stiffening up, for letting doubt take over and thwart what could have been a fun ride. I fumble to my feet and find my skis miraculously attached. Shaking, I aim the tips down, bend deep at the knees, and finish the slope, Keira finally slowed as if she understands what that last one cost.

I stop on the small wooden bridge to dig out the snow packed into the tops of my boots, and to brush it off my arms and legs. No announcements of pain issue from my body. Not even my neck, the one my doctor described as that of an eighty year old, complete with deteriorating discs and bone spurs. Just the usual voices. One telling me this is too much, I should turn around, I don't want to break a bone for my birthday. The other saying I'm past the steepest part, I shouldn't quit, it's a piece of cake from here on out.

The next section has no definable trail, but we're above tree line now, so we just head out across the base of O'Malley Ridge, steering clear of alder thickets. The sun melts the remaining snow from my clothes, and the trail slopes slightly upward. I warm up, peel off layers, wipe steam off my sunglasses. O'Malley, Tikishla, Knoya, and the rest of the Chugach tower over me to the east, their toothed ridges achingly gorgeous against a blue sky. To the west, tundra falls away to mountain hemlock and alder and then to spruce forest, and then drops off and opens up to a view of the Anchorage Bowl and Cook Inlet and the volcanic peaks of the Alaska peninsula beyond. Northward, three hundred miles away, Denali and Mount Foraker shimmer white and sharp and inviting.

Up ahead is a signpost for the Williwaw Lakes trail, which in summer heads up another valley along the northwest side of 5,100-foot O'Malley Peak to a series of crystal-clear alpine lakes. There I intersect with the ski trail, a few faint lines still visible beneath snow. Energized by the view and the warmth of the sun, comforted by the sign of a trail, I get into a rhythm and stretch out my glides, a song I'm learning on piano keeping time in my head.

On the far side of O'Malley Ridge, the snowy slope is etched with sinuous curves, two of them crisscrossing to make a near-perfect chain. Telemark skiers have scribed these lines. It was probably the two I passed near the trailhead; they probably camped at the base and hiked up to ski down, again and again, carving this vertical chain of infinity, like a strand of my own DNA. Telemark skiing—that's also on my life list.

Keira has fallen into her long-distance trot, the fluid motion that reminds me she comes from a long line of sled dogs, and before that, of wolves, who know how to move over the land for miles and miles, covering far more ground than I ever do with her. On her frequent escapes, when she's gone for most of a day or more, that's what I imagine her doing—gliding easily along, mile after mile, a steady gait.

Keira is unlike any other dog I've lived with; she's more like a cat, or a wolf; she's not entirely tame. She runs off whenever she gets the chance and never returns on her own; she will not learn to sit or stay or come. At first I fought it. I wanted an obedient, loyal, adoring dog. I wanted to put that bumper sticker on my car, the one that says *Oh Lord, help me be the person my dog thinks I am.* But now the bumper sticker lies lost in some drawer, and I want to be more like Keira—strong, independent, confident, sure of my body, unconcerned with what others think—and jubilantly wild.

I revel in the beauty with which she runs before me, as smooth and level as a Kentucky Derby champion, all in a lithe forty-five-pound body. The legs power forward and back in steady rhythm; there is no wasted movement. Those rare times I let her off leash, I vicariously bound through forest and across tundra, covering distances in an amount of time unattainable with these two legs. And when she pricks up her ears and stares intently across the landscape, I awake from my thoughts to follow her gaze, looking for what she so easily finds.

I stop to take a drink, share a granola bar with Keira, and listen. All I hear is nothing. Absolute stillness. No planes, no birds, nothing. I close my eyes, take a deep breath, turn my face to the sun, and savor it. So few times in life have I experienced absolute silence. One of the first times was in the Black Canyon of the Gunnison in southern Colorado; the quiet was finally broken by a far-off howl of coyotes.

This time the silence breaks with a shrill keening, the call of a golden eagle. A pair of them make wide circles in the brilliant sky, the sun glinting off their wings. They hover over a small peak in front of Wolverine Peak, one that we named Mount Keira. Last August, my husband and I had hiked it with Keira off-leash. Above tree line, with two of us to watch her, we agreed to take the risk, even though the thick black fur on her back and the white of her legs and belly are perfect camouflage in this land of granite and snow. Long before us, she reached the peak, then dashed down the other side. There we watched an Arctic ground squirrel gathering grass and carrying it into one of many den entrances; we found two Dall sheep, a female with a kid, nibbling lichen on the rocky ledges beneath us; and we kept watch on the small white and black spot bounding across the tundra, the one named Keira.

Skiing again, I hear the sounds: Keira's soft panting, the jingle of her tags, the swish of my skis, the puff of my poles lightly touching snow. I imagine how content I'll feel at the end of this day; how, a week or month from now, I might sit at a stoplight in Anchorage, facing the mountains, and pick out the peaks I ski by today, remembering, reliving.

I hit a downward curve and lose my balance, falling off the trail into deep snow. With my body lower than my skis, I move as awkwardly as a newborn moose trying to stand. I laugh out loud at the image, brush off the snow, and head up a hill. Then another downhill, another uphill. This trail is more of a roller coaster than I remembered. As I pause on a ridge, Keira bounds off the trail; the line disappears into deep snow, no dog in sight. I flash back to that first steep hill and the nearly painful fall. I've yet to see another human out here, and the trail looks as if it hasn't been used for days. My body tenses.

I stop at the top of a long descent and stare at the bottom, where there's a sharp right turn onto a narrow bridge across a small snow-covered stream. This looks tricky. Maybe I should take off my skis and walk. No, give it a shot. I take a deep breath, pray Keira doesn't pull too hard, and bend my knees. We sweep down the hill, carve the snow, make the turn, fly across the bridge, and glide halfway up the next hill before slowing.

"Oh, yeah!" I yell, whooping as if I had just won an Olympic medal. "Way to go, girlfriend!" I tell Keira. She looks at me, those sky-blue eyes in a symmetrical black mask surrounded by a thick white ruff—that face that elicits more compliments than a trophy wife.

We've left tundra behind and are in alder now, with patches of spruce and birch. Much of the time all I can see is the narrow path; listening becomes more important. I stop. Nothing but the sound of a distant jet on its way to Anchorage. The creek, whose muted song has come and gone throughout the day, has disappeared over a hill to navigate a valley outside my view.

As if searching for the creek, the trail takes another dive, this time into thick forest. From the trees comes another sound, a human voice. Then out ski two young men and a dog, a big Lab/shepherd mix, thundering up toward Keira. She pulls, leaping toward the black dog. I rein her in like a fish on a line, pulling her close so her leash won't trip them. One of the guys yells, "On by!" to the dog, and they power past us, nodding a quick hello, disappearing as suddenly as they appeared.

In the remaining silence, I peer down the hill. I was wrong about that first drop at the beginning of the trip. This is the steepest yet, plus it's long enough to gain plenty of speed, and it ends with a swerve to the right so sharp it vanishes from sight.

"All right, Keira," I say in a low voice, "let's take it slow."

Right. She takes off fast while I try to snowplow across the narrow trail, the backs of my skis pushed out and the front tips touching, but our speeds are so different that she quickly reaches the end of the leash and yanks me forward. For a few seconds I'm upright, hanging on like some clown in a circus act, then I pitch forward just as the trail veers right, plunging deep into snow.

Pain shoots up my leg. Ankle, knee, hip. They all hurt. I don't move, willing the pain to subside or at least identify its source. I'm not scared so much as irritated. Why couldn't I have done this without falling? Those two guys could have; they wouldn't have even bothered snow-plowing. I'm glad I passed them before I fell, but then again maybe not—maybe I'll need help. Maybe I'm not going to be able to move. Maybe no one else will ski by today, and I'll be here all night. This isn't the kind of winter camping I had in mind.

Maybe I should take Keira off the leash, so she'll go find help. But she is at the very end of the line, facing away up the trail, her back legs crouched, her body leaning forward, straining, pulling, ready to go, absolutely ignoring my fall. The score to *Lassie* dissipates. Be like Keira. Ignore the pain. Go.

I try to move. Yes, I can wiggle my toes, can move my legs, but they are in some kind of pretzel I can't untangle. One ski is off and away down the hill, the other—with foot attached—is nearly vertical into the snow. I pull off my gloves and unclip the ski, easing my ankle into a normal position. I untangle legs and feet. I try to push up, off the snow, but my hands just sink me deep into a face-plant. So I pull the nearer ski along-side my body, and push up on it. By the time I'm upright with skis on, my hands and feet are numb. But the pain has subsided. No broken bones, just some muscle pulls and sprains. The left leg throbs, the ankle and knee and hip ache, but they hold my weight.

I climb the steep hill, shaking and cold. The top of the rise is in full late-afternoon sun, so I stop. The snow on my face, down my neck, in my ears, begins to melt, making my skin tingle. A pale sliver of moon hangs over the ragged white ridgeline.

I have seen this waning moon. Last night, my son James and I sat in the hot tub and watched the moon's reflection in the water, dancing with the rippling surface. We made waves and the moon danced faster. We sat still and it swayed slowly. We took turns cupping our hands around the reflection, holding the darting moon. In that moment, the possibilities of life seemed wide-open, endless. It's what I've always believed, always counted on: that it's a new day every morning, that it's never too late to try something new, to change your life. All you have to do is be willing, and listen.

Nearer now there's a tinkling sound like a high, soft bell. Icicles hang from a spruce tree right beside me, dozens of small crystalline shapes reflecting the tree, the mountains, Keira's warm body, my flushed face. It's miraculous, this world in a drop of ice—enough to give sight to the blind, voice to the mute.

The shaking stops. My heartbeat slows. The sun's warmth soaks through the cold, and a chickadee's lilting tune wafts among the trees. My body speaks, too, and though it translates to pain, I like hearing it so clearly. No broken bones, not stranded, not lost. Not as strong, perhaps, or as skilled, as those two telemarkers, or as those two guys with the dog. But out here, skiing alongside these mountains.

That's what matters. That I'm here. That we're all here. The snow, the spruce tree, the golden eagles circling Mount Keira, the ground squirrel hibernating in its den, the Dall sheep tucked under some rock ledge, this husky with frost on her whiskers, this human plowing through the snow. All of us. Here. And it's a good thing, a new day.

The rest of the way is a gradual descent, all the ups and downs behind me now. I manage to stay in the tracks most of the time, but when I don't, I just lean forward, push hard, and get back on. I glide fast and straight, keeping up with Keira, no longer trying to slow her down, no longer snowplowing. We enter a tunnel of tall spruce trees, their dark green boughs sweeping us along and then ushering us out onto the packed main trail.

Skiing this smooth route is like hitting pavement after hours of biking on a potholed, rocky, dirt road. I slide effortlessly past several groups of hikers and skiers, surprised at how skillfully I move. Evening sunlight slices through the forest, shimmering off frosted needles, lighting the way. Keira trots before me, looking satisfied, as if she'd planned it this way all along.

How Shall I Pray?

SUSAN MARSH

WHEN THE SPIRIT MOVES ME I GO OFF BY MYSELF
TO SEE THINGS THAT I ALONE MUST SEE.
—*Wang Wei*

OOTSORE FROM A WEEK of ridge walks and restive with the need
to write, I forgo backcountry companionship in favor of a day
alone. The trail I seek is an undulating ribbon threading through
frost-green sagebrush and emerald aspens, bright wildflowers and dark
timber. I bid my husband so long and hurry out the door.

At the Cache Creek trailhead mine is the only car. The only prints
denting the dust after last night's rain are those of a lone moose. The day
spreads young and airy under a crystalline sky as I grab my portable
office, one of those multizippered nylon pouches that tourists carry to
keep their passports and money clips clutched securely to their navels.
Mine holds a pocket notebook, pencils, an eraser, and a flesh-colored
sharpener the shape of a cleanly severed nose. To sharpen a pencil you
grind the lead deep into one nostril and twist.

A bower of serviceberry wraps the trail in white floral garlands and a
chorus of bird song greets the day. Kinglet, sparrow, grosbeak, finch—
voices blend as if each territorial announcement were part of a complex
fugue. I snug the laces of my boots and the car door shuts behind me
with a satisfying finality.

My destination is a group of aspens, a half acre of ghost-gray trunks with an odd clonal characteristic: Each tree stands straight as a lamppost for twenty feet, and then it curtsies and cavorts, branches kinking and corkscrewing and pretzel-twisting toward the sky. Aspens with a sense of humor—in their presence you can't help but smile. I have not visited them in months.

A fast march takes me over spur ridges and into draws carved by intermittent creeks. On open slopes a crowd of saucer faces nods my way—arrowleaf balsamroot, a member of the sunflower family whose clear yellow blossoms and footlong silver leaves grace the lower elevations for a month beginning at the end of May. "Lower elevation" is a relative term in Jackson Hole, Wyoming. My house sits at sixty-two hundred feet and the trail erupting with balsamroot climbs to not quite seven thousand. Spring arrives shy as a pale stem under ice. A week of record warmth has the rivers gushing in a brown froth through their canyons but Claytonia still blooms in shady pockets above the Cache Creek trail, unmistakable evidence of the recent departure of snow.

My feet fly along the familiar trail. For fifteen years I've known it and had named its landmarks for the ephemera of my history in Cache Creek: Christmas Corner, Peanut Butter Point. After my Labrador retriever's sometime nickname, Butthead Butte. As I pass each personal spot I silently acknowledge it before veering from the trail. The aspens I'm aiming for grow a half mile up the mountain. I race up the hill and nearly stumble over a hidden log in my haste to reach them. The morning sun glances through their branches, aglow with the year's unfurling leaves. The last time I saw them they fluttered in the raking autumn light like stained-glass bangles of crimson and gold against the cobalt sky. But that was in October and now it's nearly June, and except for a few scant hours on skis I've spent no time outdoors alone. The resulting hunger for solitude lay restless in my heart and roosted in my thoughts as I decided how to pass this fine spring day.

Lately I've been running on worry and caffeine, my heart like a bird beating against the confining cage of my ribs. As I ease to the damp earth under the aspens' whimsical curlicues I'm invited to play in their company, to forget about being a grownup. Perhaps I'll roll around in the dewy grass or spend an hour watching the progress of an iridescent beetle, fascinated as a five year old. I rest my shoulder on a chalk-white trunk while the sweat dries from my back, motionless for long enough to become just another boulder to the ants and spiders. A ruffed grouse drums on a nearby log with accelerating thumps like a heartbeat out of control. A woodpecker taps up the trunk above me and dips away. Though I've come here by myself, I'm far from alone. Songbirds, grouse, ants, and trees—I have a host of companions. The quiet acceptance of wild, familiar things.

Anniversaries have brought me here. Four months ago I turned fifty. This is my fourth day on a drug I swore I'd never take, one of those serotonin-enhancers that's supposed to make me feel "myself" again—whomever that might be. I've completed my fourth in a series of sessions with a counselor and four months of a hatha yoga class. It is my mother's fourth month in a nursing home. She seems happy in the solitude of her dementia. She doesn't know who I am.

Four is a sacred number to certain Plains Indians; fifty is a sacred number to women in our culture. The time to reassess and reevaluate our lives. A time of hot flashes and discontent, but also of doors opening onto new possibilities and directions. A time, say several of my fifty-something friends, when you're done paying off karma and it's time to speak with your true authentic voice, come in to your own wisdom, and spend the rest of your life doing what pleases you instead of pleasing others. It all sounds great and wonderful but the truth is it requires a difficult admission: What worked ten years ago doesn't anymore. This passage feels no less bewildering than puberty.

By fifty most of us are out of practice at doing things our way instead of going with the flow, so out of practice we have to pause and consider for a moment when asked to give our preference. Restaurant? Whatever sounds good to you. Place to hike? Anywhere's fine. Our husbands and lovers and friends are used to hearing this and are startled when we change our tune. But even as we rediscover long-lost voices and opinions, we're rusty as old hinges at making time for a wander alone in the woods. I find myself matching outdoor tales with others—the day I watched from the edge of an avalanche gully while a bear used its claws like a garden rake to harvest huckleberries. A rockfall that blocked my descent from a peak and forced me to route-find in the dark. Vivid memories, but some of them happened many years ago. What have I been doing since?

Avoiding solitude, it seems. Taking it in ever-smaller doses. Solitude is a state that people in our culture can't quite come to terms with—we are loath to admit that sometimes having been to the wilderness alone appeals more than actually being there. We cherish our flirtations with solitude but at some fundamental level we must fear it, for we find unlimited excuses for dodging it. What else accounts for the proliferation of distractions, the increasing encounters I have with hikers on a forest trail yaking away with cell phones in their ears?

At fifty I have had enough distraction for a lifetime. So much that I hardly noticed when I started losing track of myself. Now I hope to find my way again. At fifty, I am ready to come home.

By *home* I don't mean the house or town or region where I live but that steadfast interior of the self, the balance the heart seeks between society and solitude. I've never found the fulcrum, even in the outdoors. Go solo or gather a group? Launch the kind of adventure one can only have alone or grasp for company in my small tribe of outdoorswomen? I used to spend enormous energy organizing hikes and river trips, yet once on the trail I often find myself tiring of company and conversation and the need for group decisions. Why didn't I just come by myself?

One reason I don't go alone is that I am weary of hearing myself talk and when I'm alone I'm the only one talking. But entering the wilderness alone offers another possibility—that of not talking. Enchantment follows silent immersion in the mysterious and ineffable wild, in whose presence the flood of words dwindles to a trickle and dries up. It's not that I don't cherish memories of trips with friends. I still laugh over the canoe expedition when the only piece of equipment we rescued from a flash flood was the ammo can that held ten days' worth of shit. But the small and intimate moments of going it alone cling to a deeper part of me.

I have let precious solitude slip away much as I have let myself-as-home slip away. Silent and unnoticed as a thread of morning fog rising from a river. For decades I've depended on solo time in the wilderness to ward off a more fearsome form of seclusion—depression, isolation, feeling socially inept in the presence of others. Working in the wilderness as an employee of the U.S. Forest Service, I once grew confident while packing trash and clearing trails and giving backpackers moleskin for their blisters. In the woods I felt valuable in ways I never have in human company. The wilderness has long been my intimate, a place where I connect with something greater, a living presence far more potent and primary than myself. It is the place where I encounter God.

Who would voluntarily sacrifice such a gift? Why have I? For one thing, I've gotten lazy. It's easy to make plans with others and hard to explain if I want to go alone. This morning my husband gave me a doubtful look, concerned about bears and transients drifting into town with the first warm winds of summer. "It's fine," I said. "I've been doing this for years." But when I left the house the seed of anxiety was planted and now it stirs in the fertile soil of my imagination. After all, it's not as if I haven't walked smack into a bear, gotten lost, or twisted an ankle on loose talus when alone. I've certainly encountered folks who made me glad I was carrying pepper spray.

A larger problem looms, one I hate to acknowledge: I've become accustomed to comfort, cautious in a vague and general way—less because of real hazards than because I've adopted the mindset of a conservative middle-aged responsible adult. This is definitely something I never meant to be.

The grass is dry and the day is warming. I remind myself that I came here to write—the latest assignment from my counselor.

A thousand impressions crowd my head and jostle for attention. Trying to capture them on the page is like finding solo time—diversions come too easily. I haven't been sitting here long enough to flatten the grass and already I feel guilty for leaving my husband on a day when we would normally be hiking together. My resolve to spend this time alone begins to fade. I'm being selfish and others need me.

But I need this. Who knows if I will feel more centered and at peace, the *chi* flowing happily, if I keep up the yoga? Who knows if my new brain drug will eliminate sudden outbursts of anger and tears? I do know this from years of practice: Solo time outdoors is balm to the soul. It pulls me out of self-absorption and frees the caged bird inside. It reassures me that my mother is safe and taken care of and that I've done the most I can for her. In the meanwhile the grand tableau of the wild world unfolds and I'm invited to participate.

A friend once mused that walking in the woods is praying with your feet. I have long subscribed to that belief, but at fifty, my feet are getting tired.

When I was a wilderness ranger I traveled in the mountains for a week at a time. I went for adventure, to prove I could hike those daily fifteen miles or climb to the top of that peak, to pack an extra bag of garbage down the trail or find my way when there was no trail. Now I no longer need to convince myself that I can overcome discomfort or fatigue or the perceived limitations of gender. I have overtaken enough buff guys on steep switchbacks (and gotten strange looks for it) to know my need for even this subtle form of competition is behind me. And that's a good thing, for truly, I'm feeling old and tired. By choice, my days alone outdoors have become a meditative spiritual practice. By necessity, now that my ankles and hips ache, my days have become shorter.

When my counselor gave me the assignment to write about why I feel at such loose and frayed ends, I had an immediate answer. "I'm fifty. Doesn't everybody feel this way?"

Only half a joke. I imagine other women drifting serenely through middle age and menopause, taking it in stride the way they have the rest of their carefully controlled lives. In most of the ways that matter I am not so different, yet I'm having trouble accepting the changes I knew were on the way. Appearing to have it all together takes more energy than it used to. Like my feet at fifty, my heart is tired.

Ten years ago I told myself that I was aging gracefully. Crow's feet and gray hair gave me a wise and weathered look. Then the muscles in my forearms began to shrink toward toothpicky flimsiness. My calves followed suit. I used my ski poles with more force and raised a barbell to the ceiling and climbed fifteen hundred feet of switchbacks up Snow King Mountain three times a week. But my arms remained skinny and my calves no longer packed their former power on the uphill trail. When my hips and knees began to creak the thought of crouching to light the camp stove was more daunting than the weight of my backpack, and I hefted it less often. I used a foam pad instead of sleeping directly on the ground "to be closer to Mother Earth," as a friend once said. I remember when he said it he was older than I am now.

All of this pisses me off. Vigorous and strong at sixty, seventy, eighty, and beyond, the older women I have known have held a torch for me. Inger still skis the Jenny Lake trail regularly at eighty-seven and

Lorraine still kayaks at eighty-two. Hazel died at a hundred and one, not long after her last of many expeditions to the Arctic. Such vitality over a long life is thanks in part to genes and constitution, but it also grows from an abiding love of wilderness and solitude, an insatiable curiosity and sense of wonder at the world. It comes from the ability to find solace in one's own company. These women have demonstrated with their lives that time alone in the wilderness improves one in ways beyond the obvious benefits of physical fitness and self-reliance. In the wilds you manage by your wits and learn more about the trees and flowers than their names. You glimpse the complex dance with which all life interrelates, a dance that includes you. Alone, you're alert and attuned and your senses open like windows on the first green day of spring, relieved that for once they don't have to withdraw to cat-eye slits in defense against the daily onslaught of too much noise and information. With practice you learn the meaning of what reaches your eyes and nose and ears: The fresh bear scat warns, the redolence of ripe berries delights.

In the wild you learn humility and gratitude. Grace and joy find you. Each time you return from a sojourn in the wild you're changed, having seen what only you could see. Each time you return the wild stays in your heart. It emerges later as humor, perspective, kindness, patience, and the desire to give without the need for thanks. This is what I see in older women whose lives have included much time outdoors alone.

I must accept, with a depth I've not yet plumbed, that my path might be different than the ways of my mentors. They didn't spend their early decades under backpacks on the trail; they followed husbands and raised children. At nineteen my job was to inventory roadless areas in the Washington Cascades and I spent a year in the wilderness. I've woven my life around the outdoors ever since and I'm paying for it now. Too many years of carrying a heavy backpack, too many turned ankles and twisted knees, too many miles off the trail scrambling in tenny-runners instead of stiff leather boots.

It took only an hour to reach my beloved stand of aspens but I fore-see the time when I won't be able to get here anymore. I have blithely assumed that of course each year I would visit my favorite wild haunts with plenty of time and energy to discover new retreats. I've looked for-ward every year to a Summer Solstice ritual, a twenty-miler off the trail with a few thousand feet of elevation gain. The only constraint is day-light and in the middle of June there are eighteen hours of it.

These days I know that each trip to a high remote peak could be my last. What made me expect I would be doing this forever? I've never quite been a jock, but my identity has nonetheless been tied to physical endurance and an ability to go wherever my feet took me. At fifty, I con-front a new reality: a body asking for rest. My first response is to bring on the usual pep talk. Meet the challenge; no whiners. Raise the barbell higher, race faster up the exercise trail. But cheerleading doesn't mask the truth. Someday I won't be doing this. Alone outdoors I find good company among the birds and wildflowers. Indoors, in the increasing isolation of old age, the prospect of being alone is something altogether different. What new solo adventure awaits the one with failing feet and ankles, grating kneecaps, and a sacrum that registers a sharp complaint each time I bend into a steep pitch on the trail?

Morning has passed and the aspens sigh in the first stirrings of an afternoon breeze. The finch and kinglet and white-crowned sparrow deliver a quiet coda to their earlier symphony and the frontal hills of the Gros Ventre Range fold together like praying hands—forested Snow King Mountain on one side, the sage- and aspen-covered hills opposite. Rendezvous and Mount Glory in the distance, all the peaks and ridges I have wandered with others and alone. Home range. Already I'm nostal-gic, wanting to recapture every day I've spent among the summit rocks and wildflowers. How will I keep these places in my heart when I can no longer skim along the rimrock with the wind, ignited by the freedom of the wilderness and falling in love again with every step? When my feet no longer carry me, how shall I pray?

When you're stuck, a famous poet once advised young writers, lower your standards. The beauty and power of the wild unsticks me, whatever my dilemma. The fanciful aspens whose lime-green leaves flutter overhead remind me that beauty is not confined to the farthest ridges. They revel in the high spring sun, heedless that they grow three miles and not thirty from the edge of town. I follow their lead and sprawl in the grass, arms akimbo and legs in a twist. I rub my hair into the smoky musk of last fall's leaves until I nearly burrow underground to join the clone of aspens at its core. The far remote may be retreating from my unassisted reach, but I can still walk to this secret place where I find fewer signs of others than at a popular destination deep in the backcountry. This is an undistinguished draw cut by a nameless intermittent creek on the unsurveyed margin of the Gros Ventre Wilderness. I'm as alone here as I would be on snowy Rendezvous today, so alone that no one would find me if I decided to stay forever.

Hang onto your curiosity, advised Mardy Murie, another mentor who recently passed away at the age of a hundred and one. Among these trees I remain endlessly curious, staring into the depthless sky or crawling in the grass with a hand lens to discover dozens of insects I've never seen before. Here I find endless rapture in the soft spring earth, the fount of all things wild. Beyond the small accomplishments of reaching a summit or paddling a river, the greater conquest is that of the ego. In the wilderness I am at my best, enchanted by all that lies on the horizon and at my feet. In the wilderness I go to the well and fill my pail with sweet cold water. Fortification for the work ahead.

Like a frosted peak in a patch of blue when the storm begins to lift, my ruminations resolve into a plan. The path ahead is dictated by my years in the backcountry, by the promises I've made while praying with my feet. I will approach the solitude of my writing desk with renewed enthusiasm and the belief that what I do there could make a difference. I will embrace the fellowship of others, sharing my wisdom and experience. Though I have benefited from elders who introduced me to the wilderness and the need to speak on behalf of that which cannot defend itself, it has never occurred to me that I might also be a mentor. Suddenly I'm filled with the flush of unconsidered possibility. This fits, like the surprising but inevitable conclusion to a well-rendered story.

My story is nothing new, only my particular rendition of the oldest story of all—the quest for understanding of the self, for consequence in one's brief passage in this world. At fifty, I can't say I'm finished paying karma but I know I'll never tire of learning and sharing what I've learned. Each time I write about the wild world I peel another layer away, coming ever closer to the core of understanding, fueling my words with the hot fire in the heart that says *this matters*. Each time I introduce others to my favorite peaks and wildflowers, the nests of birds and stories in the rocks, I help them find their own paths to deeper experience, to the inner contentment and peace that comes with reflective time outdoors. Their hearts enflamed, they'll add their voices to those who speak for the wild, in the language of renewal and hope.

How shall I pray? I have spent countless days in the wilderness filling my little pail. The time for contemplative prayer is over and urgent is the need for service. I will be enough if I've helped one eager soul discover the enchantment of wild solitude, a gift that can never be taken away.

Strata

BK LOREN

"**D**EAD *person*," my partner says. I glance up from my newspaper. "What's that, hon?" We're having a lazy evening together, listening to music, reading, and when the lyrics say something about dust and love and sweat, when they spew some semi-existentialist pop notion of skeletons and "the dead man" trying to get out of everyone, my partner says, "He should have said 'dead *person*.'"

The paper falls limp in my lap. I try to hide the vigor with which I smack the palm of my hand against my forehead and pinch the bridge of my nose between my thumb and forefinger. "Do skeletons even have gender?" I ask.

That's when it begins. When my own bones start to push through my skin and my stripped down, clenched-toothed smiling skeleton rises to the surface of me and capsizes my heart, my head, my ability to reason. Laundry? Bills? Sunday mornings in bed with a latte and the *New York Times*? Love? Suddenly I want none of these. Though I am, by nature, a semi-domestic, introverted person, today I shed my newspaper, stand from the couch, open my mouth and howl, "I need to be alone, a-lone. Ahhh-looooooone."

At least, that's what I do in my imagination. In reality, I go back to reading the newspaper, noting quietly to myself that the last straw has just drifted to light on the camel's back. My mind gallops like a dromedary to some lonely desert where sand storms will blind me and sun will burn me and I'll swoon in the magnificent discomfort of naked land and relentless weather.

But, unlike when I was younger, there's a hesitation: It's been over ten years since I walked into the wilderness alone with a backpack strapped to my back and my own little heart ticking in my suddenly resonant chest. The act of taking a solo adventure may be like riding a bicycle; you may never forget how to plan a trip, read a map and compass, or load a pack. But after a long time away from epics alone in the wild, something happens inside. To say it's a loss of courage is too easy.

The next dimension is not the fifth dimension,
not a logical extension of the fourth.

I was sixteen when I went on my first overnight camping trip alone, and my methods, to say the least, were less than savvy. I tossed a sleeping bag in the back of my VW, lied to my parents and said I was meeting a friend at her family's cabin, and took off for Moab, Utah. I was Edward Abbey's nightmare, a juvenile tourist who had just finished reading *Desert Solitaire*, and was setting off into her own romanticized version of his book with the right intentions and the wrong idea, or, more accurately, with *no* idea. I was equipped with knowledge I'd gleaned from Abbey's book, which, as I recall, included things like: "If you're thirsty in the desert, suck on some gravel; it'll stimulate your salivary glands and that will quench your thirst"; and, "If you come across a pool of clear, pristine water, don't drink it; it's likely toxic. Wait till you see the water that's full of bugs, then drink heartily. If it hasn't killed the bugs, it probably won't kill you." I didn't know, as I read, that Abbey was such a jokester.

I also didn't know (or I might have ignored) that you had to get a permit for overnight trips in a national park. I was raised in the sixties and early seventies. Freedom was just another word for nothing left to lose.

This is what I did: I drove all night to reach Canyonlands by dawn. Once there, I turned onto one of the many dirt roads that marked the desert like a woman's long hair, red or blonde, curving in waves away from the straight black highway. After traveling a mile or so, I pulled to the shoulder of the road, parked my VW, and stepped into the desert with the intention of spending a week alone. The desert, I figured, was an easy place to begin because the warm weather made it possible for me to carry just a daypack and a light sleeping bag.

When you're young, you may lack adultlike confidence, but you feel unequivocally invincible. The more angsty, angry or alienated you are, the more invincible you become. You read of a plane going down somewhere, your sixteen-year-old brain deeply believes that if *you'd* been there, *you* would have been the sole survivor. Anthony Robbins' Seminars have little appeal to you because of course you can walk across hot coals without getting burned. Only old farts are susceptible to such blockheaded notions as *logic* and *physical reality*. At sixteen, intelligence and confidence are as cool and sharp as pearl-handled switchblades that only open toward the carrier.

On my little jaunt into the desert, however, I was armed only with a Swiss Army knife. At that time, the only story I'd ever read of a woman going it alone in any kind of wilderness was *Alice's Adventures in Wonderland*. She was my model, and for the first few hours, the desert was my rabbit hole. Everything was confusing, otherworldly, and magical.

The first place I came to was a landscape of goblins. Sandstone spires about my height and girth peopled the desert floor and stood close enough together to seem like a crowd at a huge party. Here, the wide open spaces of the West vanished. This land was as thickly forested with stone as the New England woods are with trees. There was nothing growing in sight—just sand and eerie rock formations for miles.

By evening, I'd made my way out of the maze of people-sized spires and had walked into an open landscape of giant monoliths. It was dusk by then, and the harshness of the desert began to soften at the edges. The towering red rock formations looked like a congregation of gods. They had the distinct presence of something living. In the lengthening evening shadows, they bent toward each other, as if bowing. Then nightfall drained their vibrant colors and the desert cooled.

It cooled rapidly. I slipped into my sleeping bag, crossed my arms under my head, and fell asleep gazing at so many stars that the sky did not seem dark. It was marbled, a swirling blend of light and darkness.

At this point, I have to fess up. I've spent the last hour, and a small portion of the last couple of decades, trying to determine where I was on this trip. I look at maps. I've even returned there, tried to recreate my path. Nothing comes clear. I've come to believe that I can't recreate my course because I was traveling in circles. What was meant to be a five-day sally with freedom turned to an eight-day dance with fear.

I'd taken very little water with me, and by the afternoon of day two, I'd drunk from so many bug-ridden pools and rivulets that I swear I could feel the little critters crawling around on the inside of my stomach, which was cramped with hunger and nausea. I figured I'd head back, but when I tried to do so, the maze I'd come through seemed flipped on its side. The sandstone formations I'd intended to use as landmarks all looked exactly the same. I looked for the *one* that had the shape of a boat sailing on sand (it was a sea of boats) and the other *one* that looked like three leaning dominoes (the dominoes had toppled). Though I'd brought very little food with me, I carried plastic bags and two tennis-ball tubes, which I used to pick up my own shit and carry it out. On day five of heading "back to my car" I had a pack full of shit, no food, and absolutely no idea where I'd come from or how to get back.

The rest of the trip—three more days—stretches, in memory, into one long day punctuated with darkness and light. I barely slept. At one point

I sat down and wept, my back to a rock. I was so lost. I imagined, indeed I *felt* my inevitable demise, here, in the desert.

It wasn't, however, as dire a moment as it should have been. Though the possibility of my own end was very real, it didn't come to me in that way. It was dramatic, youthful, everything a theory. If I'd painted my self-portrait at that time, it would have looked a lot like Prometheus, the one who stole fire from the gods and was punished by being strapped to a rock, his chest split open to vultures for eternity because he was a demigod and could not die. I was terrified, yes, but the complexity of loss didn't sink into my bones. I believed I would survive myself, that my death would be terrifying and untimely—and that I would somehow be there to watch it. Fear sheathed my body, but just beneath it lay a fine layer of adolescent ignorance that kept whispering, "This *is* kinda cool."

A few days later, I stumbled, somehow, into the goblined landscape where I had started my journey. Even though I was that close to my car, I searched another twelve hours for my beginnings. I hadn't eaten for three days, and when my car appeared in the distance, I barely recognized it. Dust had painted it the same color as the land. It looked like yet another rock formation, the stumpy one shaped like a VW.

At the restaurant where I stopped to eat, I downed the Mason jar of salsa that sat on my table before the waitron came for my order.

I returned to civilization humbled. I figured I'd never again go into any kind of wilderness alone. But already something had broken through my fear.

As harrowing and, from this perspective, embarrassing, as my first outing was, I was hooked. The particular type of solitude that only wild land can bring had infected me. There is no other place where the seam of the world becomes more vivid, where nothing separates you from the naked beauty of life—no walls to keep weather from caressing your skin, no ceiling to mask the clouds and the wealth of real information they bring, no air conditioning or heat to make the passing of seasons a nostalgia that you long for, if only you could remember their rhythms, or even the first four notes of summer turning to fall.

Life seems more abundant and immediate when you're in the wilderness. And the flip side of this is also true. Death strolls by you with a more intimate glance. I'm not saying that I nearly died on my first trip. I didn't. But a subtle twist of fate in the outdoors can always turn one bad choice into a fatal error, and I had made a series of bad choices.

There are a couple of ways to learn; one way is traveling backwards from an experience that demonstrates what you *don't* want to do. My first solo excursion provided a syllabus to the don'ts of backpacking. I had no question about why an outdoor trip demands such planning beforehand and such attention in the moment. I had no interest in shortcuts. In those pre–Gloria Steinem days, there was little support for a gal who wanted to backpack, so I took a part-time job selling swim suits in a sporting goods store and migrated, whenever possible, to the camping and backpacking department. Though my boss reprimanded me every time he found me—a young woman!—rummaging through the JanSport packs and Coleman stoves, I persisted. Soon the store was footing the bill for me to attend all sorts of seminars on the latest equipment, technology, and outdoor safety. A year later, I'd been on several legitimate backpacking trips with the boys from work, and a couple of solo journeys.

When I used to teach writing, I suggested to my students that they begin to remember and record their dreams. I warned them, though, that writing about their dreams in fiction or nonfiction didn't usually translate well.

"Well, then why do you want us to pay attention to them?"

"Because—you spend at least a third of your life asleep. There's a whole part of yourself that you're missing, and what's missing in you inevitably ends up missing in your writing."

Walking into the wilderness alone is even bigger than dreaming. There's a whole world there that is archetypically part of who we are, but which we have pushed into unconsciousness. It becomes easy to devastate this world because we begin to believe it was never a part of us (even as we seek to name that unnamable *something* that we know could finally fulfill us). But in wilderness lies the place where life and death are more evident, more vivid, more immediate and observable. To lose this is not to lose something *other*; it is to lose the heart of who we are.

> *The next dimension rests somewhere between a point*
> *(which has the value of one) and a line (which has the value of two).*

Several years later, I began to run rivers. Once, I was on a river when a massive storm hit the land above the canyon. In Anasazi cosmogony the earth is layered like an onion, one world wrapped around another, and people emerged into this life through canyons, the *sipapu*, or womb of the earth.

Sitting at the sunny, rainless bottom of the canyon that day, watching the black lightning-cracked sky move across higher ground, I believed it. Up there was a different world, and I was watching from some inner layer of the onion.

By noon, though, the black-bellied clouds dipped over the edge of the canyon, rain crenulated the water, and the two worlds merged. The river ran metallic gray and midday dusk settled like a tight lid over the sandstone walls, turning their vibrant reds to deep mahoganies and veiny purples. Lightning lit the dark canyon like a strobe. To stay in our boats would likely have been suicide, so I followed my friends—who had run this river several times before—to the nearest beach. I was relieved to be out of the river, but my friends were agitated.

They yelled above the thunder, the rain, and the thwap of our plastic ponchos. "This is a side canyon," said Brian.

"Out of the rain," yelled Steve.

"Yeah, and if it flash floods, we're all dead."

Steve shook his head and laughed. "That's an old wives' tale."

Brian didn't mince words. He secured the boats as best he could, then gathered the group and started climbing the canyon wall. When we got to higher ground, we waited.

It rained. I mean, it rained hard enough that the sky seemed a tributary of the river—no drops on the surface, just a steady pour. A few minutes later, as smoothly as synchronized swimmers, everyone looked up. There, in a narrow spot on the canyon's rim, water shot out as if from a huge spigot. It stayed suspended, believable as a Dali painting, for some time, then suddenly exploded into a mist. A sheer white veil danced across the backdrop of red sandstone until gravity snagged a corner of it and tugged. At that moment, a waterfall appeared. I gushed through winding crevices, then crashed into the river.

That's not a typo. I didn't mean to say "*It* gushed through the crevices . . ." I'm familiar with the theory of subject-object distinction. But in the onion of the world that is wild, there is none. Indeed, the rainwater did gush through the crevices and crash audibly into the river, and at the same time, I could feel it rushing over my sandstone body, could feel my giddy self tumbling weightlessly down the bumpy, well-veined canyon. If there had been a real I present, I would have looked at my friends and smiled. As it was, none of us was anything but river and stone.

We watched waterfalls form one after the other. We watched, also, as flash floods gushed through side canyons, dumping boulders and entire trees into the roiling river. There but for the grace of angels.

That night we anchored ourselves to small ledges, and made our beds above the mouth of the side canyon. The rain had turned to a whisper, but the volume of the river was still increasing, and the narrow beach where we'd anchored our boats was calving off in huge chunks. We didn't want to wake in the morning and find ourselves up shit creek without a paddle, or raft, or kayak. So we took shifts monitoring the water level. At midnight, I sat on the narrow beach, watching the earth pull away from itself in a surprisingly sinewy way, like striated muscle pulling from bone.

This, I think, is what has been happening inside me throughout the past few years. The gradual, stormy, striated disconnect from self that happens too easily to us all.

The "fifth" dimension is the interior space between a point—one—and a line—two. It is 1.29, to be exact, and it is the dimension that describes edges, coastlines, most anything in-between.

I go about my domestic chores. I love them. I cook. I make most things from scratch. I spend time creating new recipes. I am truly interested when I slice a carrot and see the mandala there that looks like the iris of an orange human eye.

I garden. I care for my aging parents. I take them pot roasts. I visit my mother in the nursing home I swore against when I was younger and I believed all things were conquerable and that degenerative diseases only hit people who had lived "unhealthy" lives. When my father says something like "George W. Bush is a smart man," I may still drop my jaw in disbelief, but my dad's eyesight is poor enough now that he just thinks I'm yawning, and I refrain from listing, in a very loud voice, the evidence that suggests Dubya's thinking might be just a few clowns short of a carnival.

I am a woman I never thought I would be. I hike on weekends. Though I live only a few miles away from Eldorado State Park, one of America's classic rock climbing areas, I can't recall the last time I went for a climb. I run in the summer. I mountain bike and swim. I snowshoe in winter. Occasionally, I cross-country ski. I have an all-wheel drive Subaru station wagon. I could be a soccer mom, if I had kids.

My car has a CD player in it, and sometimes I blast the speakers with modern rock—The White Stripes, Tori Amos, Jimmy Eat World—and other times, I pop in an oldie.

Recently, even when I'm listening to Sylvia Poggioli and the latest NPR report, I hear Bob Dylan. He's stuck on the old forty-five player in my head, and he sings about endless road trips and twists of fate and idiot winds, and then he sings this one line that hits hard. It's about aging and desire and learning to "turn it off," the result of which is growing too "soft."

The needle skips, then lands back on the same lyric, over and over. He's singing, I think, about a lost love. I'm hearing a song about love lost. These are two different things.

Bob's gnarly voice becomes the soundtrack for the memory of two weeks I spent alone in Yosemite—ten years ago. Though one of my greatest backpacking or river-running pleasures is to mark the day when pop lyrics and commercial jingles stop playing in my head, this song accompanies the whole memory, and I welcome it. In it, I'm thirty-some years old again, and I've learned, at last, how to go safely alone into the wilds. I take food for a few extra days, and then some to share in case I come across someone in trouble—say, a sixteen year old looking for freedom. In Yosemite, I was glad to have the surplus, because the second to the last day of the trip, the trail passed by a mountain lake that was blue and sweet as a raspberry Popsicle. I mean, I could have eaten this lake whole, felt the coolness of it wash over the bitter, sweet, salty edges of my tongue, felt it shudder orgasmically through my body. Yes, it was love at first sight—not a one-night stand—and I could not bring myself to leave.

We got intimate pretty quickly. Within the first few minutes, I stripped down to nothing and submerged my body into that wide-open body of water. My heart felt like a fist slamming against the inside of my rib cage at first, a reaction to the cold. Then the lake and my skin agreed on an in-between temperature. I swam to a rock, lifted myself onto it, and sat there, naked under the wide sky, feeling the sharp, high-altitude sun like needles on my bare skin. I stayed until the twilight turned the white clouds to saffron and the lake swallowed them in. I swam back to shore in water the color of soft fire, and still it was icy cold, and still it filled me with warmth.

How long has it been since I've felt myself submerged in the world like this? How long since I reconfirmed my body as a mere swatch of this land, this land as the foundation of my being?

I stayed in that place for three days—didn't hike, didn't play hacky-sack, didn't read a book or write in a journal. I ate, slept, swam. I stayed naked the whole time. I lay on the earth. I felt the line between the earth and my body turn to seams, then felt the seams dissolve. I felt like my old VW, left for so long in one place that I became a lump of earth myself. It *felt* good to me. It felt *good* to me. It felt good to *me*.

I keep driving my Subaru wagon, and the music keeps playing, and this memory—recurring, vivid, relentless—was originally an ecstatic escape; but it turns now to agitation. I can feel the domesticity I've accumulated over the years. It's hanging from me like dust and love and sweat, and there's definitely a dead man (person? woman?) trying to get out of me.

The corpse inside me looks like fifteen years of sleeping with the same person, every night, night after night, waking in the morning to that same sameness, going to see my mom at the nursing home, listening to her roommate clear the phlegm from the tube in his trachea, watching my mother's body writhe in its wheelchair, reminding her she must keep her seat belt locked at all times, taking my father to dialysis, watching the blood be drained from his body, purified, then pumped back into his veins, searching through many exciting recipes, making a shopping list, collecting my coupons and recycled grocery bags, driving to the grocery store, buying food, coming home and shoving the food in cupboards and the refrigerator, wondering if I will ever make enough money to buy a new fridge because this one barely freezes ice cream and eggs rot in it within a week, which is quaint and interesting when you're a grad student, but I have a Subaru station wagon now, and parents who depend on me, and I have not only *known* someone consistently for fifteen years, I have slept with her over and over and have not slept with anyone else and I brush my teeth with her and eat dinner and hike and laugh and fight and own a dog and a cat, and the dog has epilepsy and I give it medication, and we (my partner and I, not my dog) are right now redoing our bathrooms and are really excited about getting rid of that vanity in favor of a white pedestal sink. In the mornings I turn on my space heater in my office because "it's just a little chilly in there," and what the hell happened to the ice-cold water and the way it made my skin turn blue and my nipples shrink to little chocolate-chip nubs, and where is that saffron sky and that evening sun, and why is my body suddenly seamless only with some kind of upholstery in some kind of office or vehicle, and Oh, thank God, finally I have enough time to sit down in a chair and listen to music and read, and just then my partner of fifteen years says to me, "Dead person," and I say "What?" and she says, "He should have said dead person trying to get out," and I think, *No, I can't do this anymore. No.*

Chaos theory has proven that it's not extending beyond that offers a new dimension; it's falling into. In the space between a point and a line, a new world unfolds.

It is a country within a country, the place I choose to go now. It is in the poorest county in the nation, Shannon County. The Pine Ridge Sioux Reservation, South Dakota.

There's no such thing as a backcountry permit on a reservation but I know some folks who know the land. I first came here over twenty years ago with my high-school friend Janice Black Elk, granddaughter of the esteemed Oglala holy man who is the subject of the book *Black Elk Speaks*. She'd been taken from her family by the U.S. government when she was an infant and was adopted by a white working-class family in my home town. We ditched out of a good portion of our senior year to travel up to Pine Ridge in search of her roots.

The border of the place has not changed much. Whiteclay, the last American town before you cross over into the sovereign nation, is as violent a place as I can imagine. It is deathly still. It consists of one condemned "inn" (I can't imagine it ever housed a traveler), one defunct auto-parts store, an auto junkyard, and two small liquor stores that tout multimillion-dollar profits. In other words, it is a town made up of the two things responsible for the premature deaths of so many Lakota people: cars and liquor. The stores are small and gray, their arched doorways the only light in this otherwise-ghost town.

Whiteclay is about two miles long, and across its entire length Lakota men and women lie in the street, sleeping, unconscious. Or they sit, drinking, with their backs against the walls of the crumbling buildings. The Sioux (Lakota) Nation has outlawed the sale of liquor on the reservation. But Whiteclay is America.

It has always been hard for me to cross this border into Pine Ridge. Once inside the reservation, however, things change. Big Bat's convenience store is a sort of reservation social hub. It is lively as any late-night grub store in Smalltown, America; but it is also another world. Trash bins and restroom signs are written in Lakota and English, and the dominant language is a blend of the two.

Behind Big Bat's and the village of Pine Ridge, land—relatively untouched prairie—stretches for miles. At the north edge of the prairie, the Black Hills (*Paha Sapa*) rise up. I've been given permission to hike in an unnamed territory of the hills. There are no maps, but I know the place well enough—have hiked it before with Lakota friends. It's not a long trip I'm planning. I want at least two nights out, simple and easy as that.

Except it is not simple.

The sight of *Paha Sapa* after so long away braces me like a cold gust of wind on a too-hot day. The hills rise up starkly. Though from a distance they appear black, they're actually wind-eaten limestone, whitish-gray, virtually barren. They look like bones that have pushed through the green, fleshy breast of the earth. The edge of the prairie folds over them like skin.

The first few steps I take into the hills are nothing short of bliss. The jabber in my head quiets almost immediately. It's the kind of terrain where you expect to see coyotes loping, tongues dangling, and that beleaguered, tough-kid look in their eyes. The limestone is the perfect camouflage for them, too. Mottled gray, unshadowed.

After about an hour, though, the starkness gives way to a grove of aspen, and the temperature drops a few degrees. This is the reason I came. A quiet attention settles into me. There's no reason to talk. No reason to reason. Sensing becomes everything.

There are a few things that could jar me out of this calm. Gunshots, for instance, might do it. Gunshots in the distance popping like the Fourth of July would even be enough. But the gunshots I hear now are not at a distance. There's a *ping* followed by a piercing-quick little doppler-effect—the way guns sound in old Westerns, as opposed to the way they sound in today's high-tech flicks. When I round the bend, I'm suddenly face to face with a Lakota man and his horse. He carries a shotgun in one hand, a pistol in a waist holster, and he's got the horse on a lead. Though it's midsummer, he's wearing a flannel shirt and Lee jeans. He speaks in a way I'm familiar with, clipped syllables, words lingering in the back of his throat.

"This is Lakota land," he says.

I stumble. I point back to where I started from. "I have some friends . . ."

"Seen any bear?" He cuts me off.

"I . . . I haven't. No." I know he knows this place better than I, but this just doesn't seem like the time or habitat where I'd see bear.

He points with his shotgun. "Seen some bear up there. If I were you," he pauses and checks me out from head to toe. "If I were you, I'd be careful."

I nod, thinking, "*Some* bear? Like, a herd?"

"You planning on camping?" he asks.

"Well, yeah, I was."

He checks me out again, then tugs the horse's lead. "Some burial lands over there." He takes a few steps. "I'd be careful if I was you." Then he continues. When he's less than five minutes away from me, the gunshots start up again.

It's more than a warning, and it throws me into a quandary. If I were in my own country, and if he were some macho guy telling me what to do, I'd ignore him and move on. But from the outset, I was a little nervous about hiking on the Pine Ridge side of *Paha Sapa*. It seemed perfect, in some ways, and disrespectful in others. But I was drawn to a land within a land, to the borders that could separate me further from my daily life. I walk a bit more, but my conscience gets to me. Before noon, I turn back.

I spend that night in a motel outside the reservation. There's an American flag on the front lawn of the place, and when you pull open the lobby door "The Star-Spangled Banner" blares until the door falls shut. I keep to my room, and I chalk up yet another thing keeping me from my desire to take some time alone in the wilderness.

I long for the days when I was younger and had more time to myself. I want—I need—to be out where I know my decisions matter, where if I make a bad choice it could mean my life. It's the tug between the exact silence of the wilderness and the specific tension that accompanies it— the one that makes me more aware of my own mortality, and thus of my own downright responsibility—that I crave. And I fear I've lost it. As any good existential philosopher will tell you, an embodied knowledge of your own mortality casts a light onto your own most authentic choices. I want to reconnect with these choices—not be bogged down in whether to paint my new bathroom mocha or mauve.

The next morning I leave my room key and a check on the counter (no credit cards, please) and "The Star-Spangled Banner" sends me on my way. I cross the reservation and come out on the other side, still the sacred *Paha Sapa*, but the American part of them that was literally filched from Sioux ownership in a recent breach of treaty.

I just don't give a shit anymore where I sleep, as long as it's outside. I mean, there is a real difference between day hiking and sleeping overnight on the bumpy earth. I have enough provisions for five days, and dammit, I've decided to sleep under the stars for every one of them. Though after my first outdoor fiasco, I've never had any serious outdoor mishaps, I almost wish for one now. I pray for sudden, severe weather. Or perhaps a slight miscalculation on my part. I want something, anything, that tests me in *that* way because my growing fear of being tested in that way has kept me from coming here. Over time, it has settled into me like a disease. It has weakened me, separated me from who I am.

Nothing like that happens. No bad weather, no bad decisions, not even any more men with guns. I hike back toward Deerfield Lake. Everything comes easily. I set up my tarp. I sleep under the stars. I make my way on unmarked trails using a map and compass. I eat peanut butter and jelly and goat cheese and bread and a little bit of gritty dirt on the side. I smell the sweet scent of aspen, the acrid hint of limestone. My senses are drenched and satiated.

In fact, on this trip, I don't feel tested in any way, and yet, it occurs to me on day three that my mind is clear and sharp anyway. I'm aware in the way I have longed for—that open-pored attention I developed over time, and which my first wilderness trips were the training ground for.

Let me stop here and say this: Long ago, I would not have ended a sentence in a preposition like that! And it occurs to me now that it's not some great internal piece of me that's missing, but rather, it is exactly this kind of niggly precision that seems to have calved off and dropped away from me altogether. I thought I'd forgotten how to go into the wild alone, but here I am, easing my way from day to day, and it's second nature for me. I realize, finally, that I did not need to relearn how to do this; I needed to reform the reasons why I do it. It is, no longer, a way to confirm my strength, perseverance, or awareness of mortality. Those things are indubitably clear to me. They are permanent.

I garden. I take out the trash. I visit my parents. I carry on an old, long-term relationship. These things look easy as hell when you're sixteen. They are not easy.

For instance, one of the things facing me now is this: My mother has Parkinson's. As she progresses further, she will suffer. She has asked me to be present if she chooses to, as the Hemlock Society says, "hasten her own death."

Maybe it's because I used the wilderness as a training ground when I was younger that I can move through these days with some degree of presence and grace. It's true—in the wilds, if you make the wrong decision, it could mean your life. But through being there, in the presence of mind demanded by wilderness, I learned that in your daily life, if you make the wrong decision, you will not die. You'll simply have to live with it.

This is what the testing ground was all about. To be present. To remain. It is far more cool and radical than being fascinated with my own death at age sixteen. These days, I've seen my fair share of death; I'm fascinated with life.

By day four, I'm blissfully saturated in weather and the bony terrain feels literally skeletal to me; I mean, I can feel it inside my skin. At the same time, I'm thinking of my home. It's a nice blend, the wild and the domestic, this place in between that allows for both, this growing-up that I almost confused with giving up.

On the way home from Pine Ridge, I stop by the nursing home. It's too late to go inside, so I sit in the lot for some time, looking up to Mom's second-floor window, thinking of the war going on in her brain. There are five stages of Parkinson's. She's passed through *onetwothreefour* of them. She's bound to a wheelchair now, restrained with a seat belt, and her body is either frozen, or it moves spasmodically, as if she's dancing off-rhythm. When she reached stage five, the doctor cut back on her meds because they would no longer help. Since then, her personality has returned.

When I visited her on my way out of town she had scrolled her radio dial randomly till it landed on the local rock station. I walked in, saw her writhing in her chair, heard the Red Hot Chili Peppers screaming, and quickly turned off the stereo.

Her body stopped moving. "What'd you do that for?" she asked.

"You liked it?"

She rolled her eyes, then scooted herself to the stereo, turned it on, and started dancing in her chair again. "Come on," she said, reaching out her hand. "It's good music."

These are among the decisions I have to make daily. To help this woman live. To help this woman die.

I arrive home sometime after midnight. My father's big red truck with its bright American flag on the aerial is parked in my driveway, which lets me know Lisa has probably taken him to the hospital again. My dog greets me at the door and my cat claws at my dog because of all the tail wagging. My body is exhausted, jittery from the drive. I don't even brush my teeth or take off my clothes. I climb the stairs, turn back the blankets, and sit on the edge of the bed. I listen to the rhythm of Lisa's breathing. She sleeps soundly. A freight train could pass through this room and she would not wake up. Still, when I say, into the darkness, away from her sleeping, "I'm home," she turns, opens her eyes. That my voice, soft as it is, rouses her from dreams, amazes me, fills me, and yes, even after fifteen years, surprises me.

This—my mother's suffering and ecstasy, my father's big red truck, my sweet epileptic dog, my cat clawing my dog, my newly remodeled bathroom, my chilly office, my love of long, lazy trips alone in the wilderness, Lisa sleeping next to me when I return home—this is my life, my mid-life to be exact, and I fall into it whole heartedly. It is my coastline, my one-point-two-nine, the place where my world grows into another dimension. It has nothing to do with extremes or going beyond. It has to do with falling. In.

Biographical Notes

Dorothy Albertini lives and writes in the Hudson Valley, where she is a research associate at the Human Rights Project at Bard College. She received her degree in creative writing from Bard; this is her first published essay.

Nancy Allyn Cook lives in McCarthy, Alaska, and received her MFA in Nonfiction Writing from the University of Alaska Fairbanks in December 2003. During the past decade, she has worked as a park ranger, backpacking guide, and outdoor educator for the nonprofit Wrangell Mountains Center. She also spent six winters serving as a National Marine Fisheries Service biologist and roe technician in the Bering Sea pollock fishery. Nancy now directs the annual Wrangell Mountains Writing Workshop. In winter, she teaches writing at the Prince William Sound Community College and University of Alaska Fairbanks. Her poems and prose appear in *Mountain Gazette, A River Teeth: A Journal of Nonfiction Narrative, Anchorage Daily News,* and *Slightly West.* She has also published interpretive and scientific documents through the Alaska Natural History Association and U.S. Fish and Wildlife Service. Her essay "Zero Degrees Fahrenheit" won the Northern Lights Essay Contest for spring 2003.

Barbara J. Euser is a former political officer with the Foreign Service of the U.S. Department of State. As a director of the International Community Development Foundation, she has worked on projects in Bosnia, Somaliland, Zimbabwe, and Nepal. She is the author of *Children of Dolpo, Somaliland, Take 'Em Along: Sharing the Wilderness with Your Children*; coauthor with Carl Blaurock of *A Climber's Climber: On the Trail* *with Carl Blaurock*; and editor of *Bay Area Gardening*. She was twenty-one when she spent the night in her solo snow cave; she is now fifty-four. She has two grown daughters and lives near San Francisco with her husband.

In 1999, **Elyse Fields** left her job as an agricultural journalist to become a park ranger, and she has since worked at Wind Cave National Park, Glacier, and the Blue Ridge Parkway. In the off-season, Elyse studies and teaches nonfiction writing at the University of Iowa, where she is completing her MFA. Her work has appeared in *Fugue*, the *Inlander*, *YES! Magazine*, as well as many local publications.

Annie Getchell has pursued big land- and seascapes on foot, on skis, and in small boats and sailing vessels. She has written for many national magazines and cohosted the PBS-TV adventure series, *Anyplace Wild*. Author of *The Essential Outdoor Gear Manual*, she has broken and repaired mountains of equipment, and of late has worked on sustainable development projects in Scotland's Outer Hebrides. Annie watches the weather from her home on the wild Atlantic coast of Donegal, Ireland.

Brianne Goodspeed received her BA in Comparative Literature from the University of Massachusetts Amherst in 2002. Since then, she has taught kindergarten, tutored immigrants in English, and worked as a caretaker in Vermont's Green Mountains. She lives in Northampton, Massachusetts.

Geneen Marie Haugen's work appears in numerous anthologies and journals, among them *American Nature Writing 2000; Another Wilderness: Notes from the New Outdoorswoman; High Country News; Solo: On Her Own Adventure; Ring of Fire: Writers of the Yellowstone Region; Alaska Passages: 20 Voices from above the 54th Parallel; Alligator Juniper;*

and *Heart Shots: Women Write about Hunting*. She's a contributor to the syndicated column "Writers on the Range" and has recently completed a young-adult novel. A two-time recipient of the Wyoming Arts Council literary award for "writing inspired by nature," she has also received writers' residencies from Ucross Foundation, Hedgebrook, and Soapstone. A longtime backcountry skier, backpacker, off-trail hiker, and river runner, she lives in Kelly, Wyoming.

Marybeth Holleman is author of *The Heart of the Sound: An Alaskan Paradise Found and Nearly Lost, The State of the Sound 2003*, and *Alaska's Prince William Sound*. Her essays, poetry, and articles have appeared in the *North American Review, Orion*, the *Christian Science Monitor, Ice-Floe, Sierra, National Wildlife, American Nature Writing, Under Northern Lights, Solo*, and the *Seacoast Reader*. She also teaches creative writing and women's studies at the University of Alaska. Raised in the Appalachian mountains of North Carolina, nearly twenty years ago she transplanted to Alaska, where she lives in the foothills of the Chugach Mountains with her husband and son.

Gena Karpf was born in Nebraska and is a current resident of Australia. She was first introduced to the wilderness at the age of eighteen during a canoeing trip to Quetico Provincial Park in Ontario, Canada. Since then, while her professional life has taken her through careers in hair-dressing, youth work, and marketing in the United States, Canada, and Australia, Gena has continued to seek opportunities for outdoor wilderness adventures. In Australia, Gena has hiked extensively and explored canyons in the Blue Mountains of New South Wales, completed the 240-kilometer Great North Walk, and plans one day to return to the Pacific Crest Trail to finish what she started. This is Gena's first published work.

A native of Washington, D.C., **Kathryn Kefauver** has lived and worked in Australia, China, and Laos, and has traveled by bike or by foot through Nepal, Italy, and Alaska. Her stories have been published in the *Gettysburg Review*, *The Journal*, and the *Christian Science Monitor*, and in 2003 she won an Associated Writing Programs award for nonfiction. She lives in San Francisco, where she is working on a novel and completing an MFA in Creative Writing at the University of San Francisco.

Holly Keith is a bookseller in western Massachusetts. She has climbed in North America, Asia, and Africa. She is also a marathon runner, distance cyclist, rock climber, and skier.

Gretchen Legler is associate professor of Creative Writing at the University of Maine at Farmington. Work from her first collection of essays, *All The Powerful Invisible Things: A Sportswoman's Notebook*, has won two Pushcart Prizes, and it has been widely excerpted and anthologized in venues including *Orion*, *Uncommon Waters*, *Another Wilderness*, *Gifts of the Wild*, *Minnesota Seasons*, *A Different Angle*, and more. Her scholarly work on American women nature writers and ecocriticism has appeared in journals and anthologies including *Studies in the Humanities*, *Interdisciplinary Studies in Literature and the Environment*, *Reading under the Sign of Nature*, and *Writing the Environment*. She is at work on a book of essays about Antarctica, where she spent six months in 1997 as a fellow with the National Science Foundation's Artists and Writers Program.

For almost a decade, **Mary Loomis** has made her home in the towns and cities throughout the Rockies. She works as a guide and educator in different mountain ranges and climbing areas in the Western United States.

BK Loren's work has garnered national awards, including the Mary Roberts-Rinehart Award, a Colorado Council on the Arts Literature Fellowship, and the Dana Award in the Novel. She is the author of *The Way of the River: Adventures and Meditations of a Woman Martial Artist*, and her work has appeared or is forthcoming in various anthologies and periodicals, including *Orion, Parabola, Two in the Wild*, and *Utne*. She lives in Colorado and is completing a novel.

Susan Marsh lives in Jackson Hole, Wyoming. Her work has appeared in *Orion, North American Review, American Nature Writing*, and the *Talking River Review*, and has been anthologized in collections including *The Mountain Reader, Ring of Fire, The Leap Years*, and *Women Runners*. Her books include *A Visitor's Guide to the Wyoming Range, Beyond the Tetons*, and *Stories of the Wild*. She is the winner of the 2003 Neltje Blanchan Memorial Award (awarded annually by the Wyoming Arts Council for literature inspired by nature).

Jennifer Mathieu was born and raised in the suburbs of Washington, D.C., and now lives in Houston, Texas. She has worked as an award-winning newspaper reporter in Houston, Miami, and Kansas City, and she has published in the feminist magazines *BUST* and *Bitch: Feminist Response to Pop Culture*. Jennifer now works for the Houston theater company Infernal Bridegroom Productions as director of marketing and development, and she is at work on a collection of essays about growing up in a family of Cuban and Chilean immigrants.

Jody Melander has lived in Provincetown, Massachusetts, for twenty years. She has been an environmental educator, artist, housepainter/carpenter, museum-store manager, grocery store clerk, whale researcher, and waitress. She has explored Cape Cod and its surrounding waters by kayak, sailboat, snorkel, rollerblades, and on foot, and is at work on a book about her adventures. This is her first published work.

Dawn Paul is a skier, sea kayaker, four-season backpacker, and writer whose stories have appeared in the anthologies *A Woman's Touch* and *Steady as She Goes: Women's Adventures at Sea*. Her play, *The Nest*, was a winner in the New Voices 2002 Annual 10-Minute Play Competition. She has written articles on science, sports, and the outdoors for *Sojourner*, *Atlantic Coastal Kayaker*, *Sea Kayaker*, and *Explore Magazine*. She teaches creative writing and poetry and is the owner and editor of Corvid Press, a small literary press. She lives north of Boston.

Sherry Simpson is the author of *The Way Winter Comes* and she teaches creative nonfiction at the University of Alaska Anchorage. She grew up in Juneau and worked for years as a reporter there and in Fairbanks. Her essays and articles have appeared in *Sierra*, *Backpacker*, *Creative Nonfiction*, *Alaska Quarterly Review*, and numerous anthologies. She is working on a group of essays about connections among wilderness, home, and the stories we find and make about our journeys. She lives in Chugiak with her husband.

About the Editor

Susan Fox Rogers is the editor of ten anthologies, including *Solo: On Her Own Adventure*, *Two in the Wild: Tales of Adventure from Friends, Mothers, and Daughters* (Vintage), and *Alaska Passages: 20 Voices from Above the 54th Parallel* (Sasquatch Books). She received her MFA in creative nonfiction from the University of Arizona, and now teaches at Bard College, where she is a member of the Institute for Writing and Thinking. She was selected by the Antarctic Artists & Writers Program to participate in the U.S. Antarctic Program during the 2004–2005 austral summer.